This Book Belongs to

SCAN TO VISIT MY AUTHOR PAGE

Join our Ministry group on facebook

https://www.facebook.com/groups/myholytrinity.co

Check out our merch at

https://fashionsbyfelicia.myecomshop.com

This book is dedicated to my Dad who taught me to be an independent and

determined person, without whom I would never be able to achieve

my dreams

ABOUT THE AUTHOR

Hello, God's children my name is Felicia Patterson,

I hold a degree in psychology, aromatherapy as

well as am an Ordained Minister. Journaling has

helped me through some very tough times in my

life along with my faith and I thought why not

combine the two. I could go on about my

accomplishments but instead, I would like to share

with you a personal story of what the power of faith

and prayer can do.

ABOUT THE AUTHOR

I was born with a rare spinal condition. My parents reached out to all the greats, but all said there was no treatment and just keep me comfortable until my time came. After months of searching and praying, a young and brilliant neurosurgeon came up with a plan that would hopefully work. Prior to what was to be a series of surgeries, I wanted to see the Happy Hunters that were a few hours away from us. Things were tight but my parents made it happen but only had fifty dollars to travel on. We got to the motel got cleaned up and walked across the street where they were giving the sermon. At this time, I had lost all function of my lower extremities and I had to be carried into the church. Prior to the sermon, they were passing the plate. We only had enough to get back home, so we don't have anything to spare. As they were passing the plate my mom put the fifty dollars in. The lady minister whom I will never forget asked my dad to sit me beside her. While her husband was giving the sermon, she was rubbing my back. My parents had communicated with them through email, but she had no knowledge of who we were or my condition. After a while, she asked my mom and another woman to take my hands and walk me around the church. I had not walked in months yet practically ran around the church. After it was over, we were headed for the lobby when the same woman that walked with me around the church came up to my mom and said, "God told me to give you this" and gave her two twenties and a ten. Our Life is a testament that through all the challenges, loss, and despair that we must hold to our faith and trust that we are all here for a purpose.

Table of Contents

Table of Contents

About your journal

Scripture

Journal

Reflect

Prayers

THE NEXT FEW PAGES WILL EXPLAIN HOW TO

USE YOUR JOURNAL

PSALMS 102

Hear my prayer, Lord;
let my cry for help come to you.
Do not hide your face from me
when I am in distress.
Turn your ear to me;
when I call, answer me quickly.
For my days vanish like smoke;
my bones burn like glowing embers.
My heart is blighted and withered like grass;
I forget to eat my food.
In my distress I groan aloud
and am reduced to skin and bones.
I am like a desert owl,
like an owl among the ruins.
I lie awake; I have become
like a bird alone on a roof.
All day long my enemies taunt me;
those who rail against me use my name as a curse.
For I eat ashes as my food
and mingle my drink with tears
because of your great wrath,
for you have taken me up and thrown me aside.
My days are like the evening shadow;
I wither away like grass.
But you, Lord, sit enthroned forever;
your renown endures through all generations.
You will arise and have compassion on Zion,
for it is time to show favor to her;
the appointed time has come.
For her stones are dear to your servants;
her very dust moves them to pity.
The nations will fear the name of the Lord,
all the kings of the earth will revere your glory.
For the Lordwill rebuild Zion
and appear in his glory.
He will respond to the prayer of the destitute;
he will not despise their plea.
Let this be written for a future generation,
that a people not yet created may praise the Lord:

Scripture

Each week 52 total plus a bonus features a new Scripture to reflect your thoughts on throughout the week giving you time to memorize the verse and understand its true meaning

ROMANS 5:8

"GOD DEMONSTRATES HIS OWN LOVE FOR US IN THIS: WHILE WE WERE STILL SINNERS, CHRIST DIED FOR US".

16

Week of:

Lord Thank You

♥ Teach Me ♥

♥ Guide Me ♥

Journal

What week is it? Record the date and watch how your journey with Gods grows through the year.

What areas of your life you want to grow? Ask god to teach me.

Let God know how grateful you are. What are you thankful for this week?

What are some areas you need God's guidance? Ask for him to guide you.

Reflect

Each week also contains a "Reflect" page with questions and thoughts inspired by the weekly Scripture, as well as room to write down your thoughts. You can use this as a weekly reflection or just fill in the blanks in a single day! Remember that this journal can be customized to fit your spiritual journey.

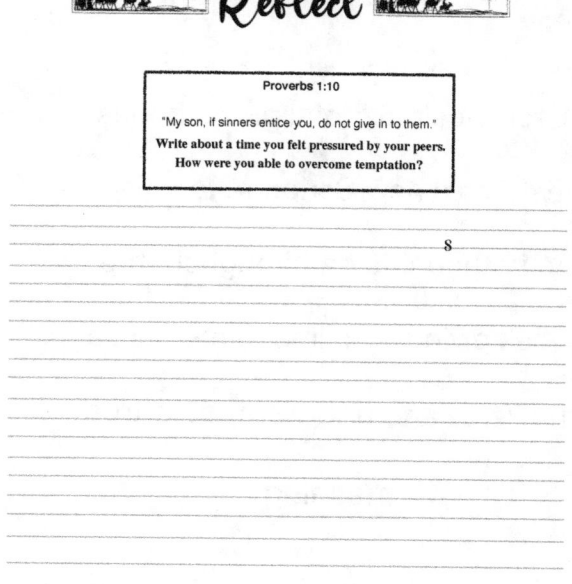

Memories, Prayers and Guidance

It's our job to guide the next generation. What do you want the future generation to know?

Record your weekly prayers.

Life is a beautiful and challenging journey. Take time to write about the

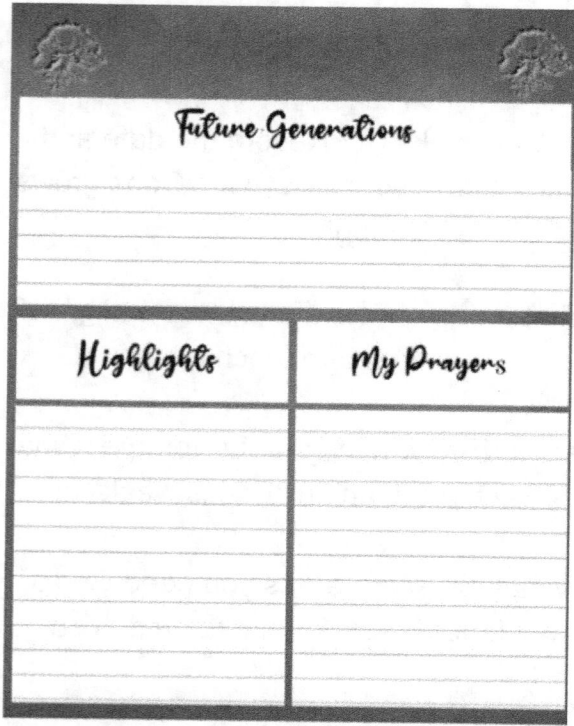

Prayers

The back of the book includes a place to record your prayers.

Now that you know how to use your journal, trust that the Lord will guide you with the year ahead.

JOHN 3:16

"FOR GOD SO LOVED THE WORLD

THAT HE GAVE HIS ONE AND ONLY

SON, THAT WHOEVER BELIEVES IN

HIM SHALL NOT PERISH BUT HAVE

ETERNAL LIFE".

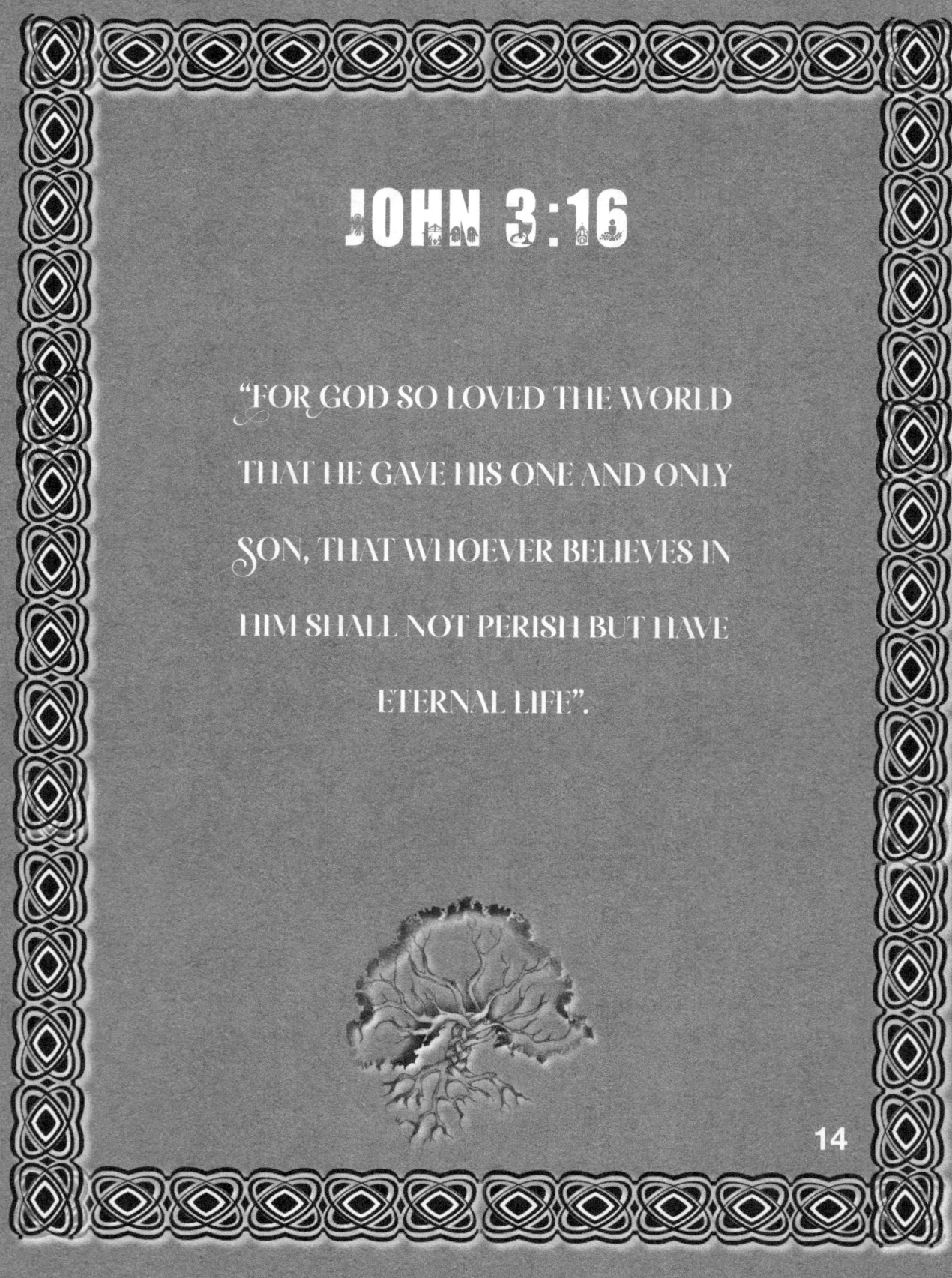

Thank You Lord

Week of: _____

Teach Me

Guide Me

 # Reflect

Proverbs 1:10

" My son, if sinful men entice you, do not give in to them."

Write about a time you felt pressured by your peers.
How were you able to overcome temptation?

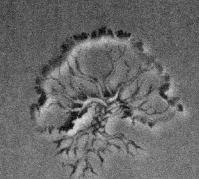
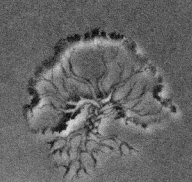

Future Generations

Highlights

My Prayers

ROMANS 5:8

"GOD DEMONSTRATES HIS OWN

LOVE FOR US IN THIS: WHILE WE

WERE STILL SINNERS, CHRIST DIED

FOR US".

Thank You Lord

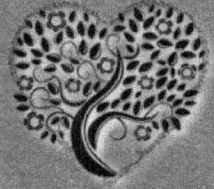

Week of: _____

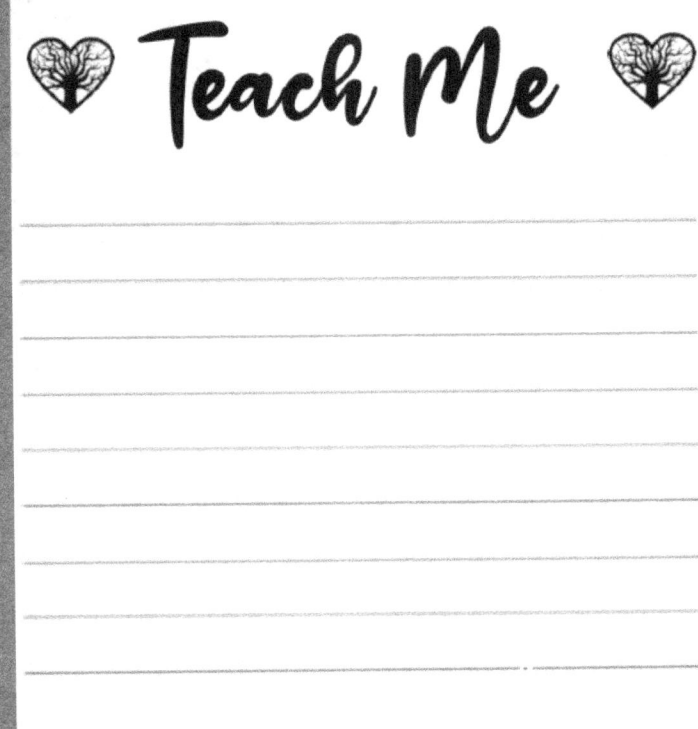

❤ Teach Me ❤

_____
_____
_____
_____
_____
_____
_____
_____
_____
_____
_____
_____

❤ Guide Me ❤

_____
_____
_____
_____
_____
_____
_____
_____
_____
_____

 # Reflect

Proverbs 1:8-9

"Listen, my son, to your father's instruction and do not forsake your mother's teaching. They will be a garland to grace your head and a chain to adorn your neck."

Write about some important advice your parents have given you that has helped

you in life.

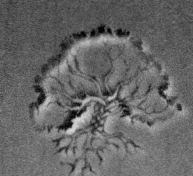
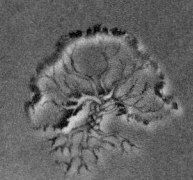

Future Generations

Highlights

My Prayers

DEUTERONOMY 31:6

"BE STRONG AND COURAGEOUS.

DO NOT BE AFRAID OR TERRIFIED

BECAUSE OF THEM, FOR THE LORD

YOUR GOD GOES WITH YOU; HE

WILL NEVER LEAVE YOU NOR

FORSAKE YOU".

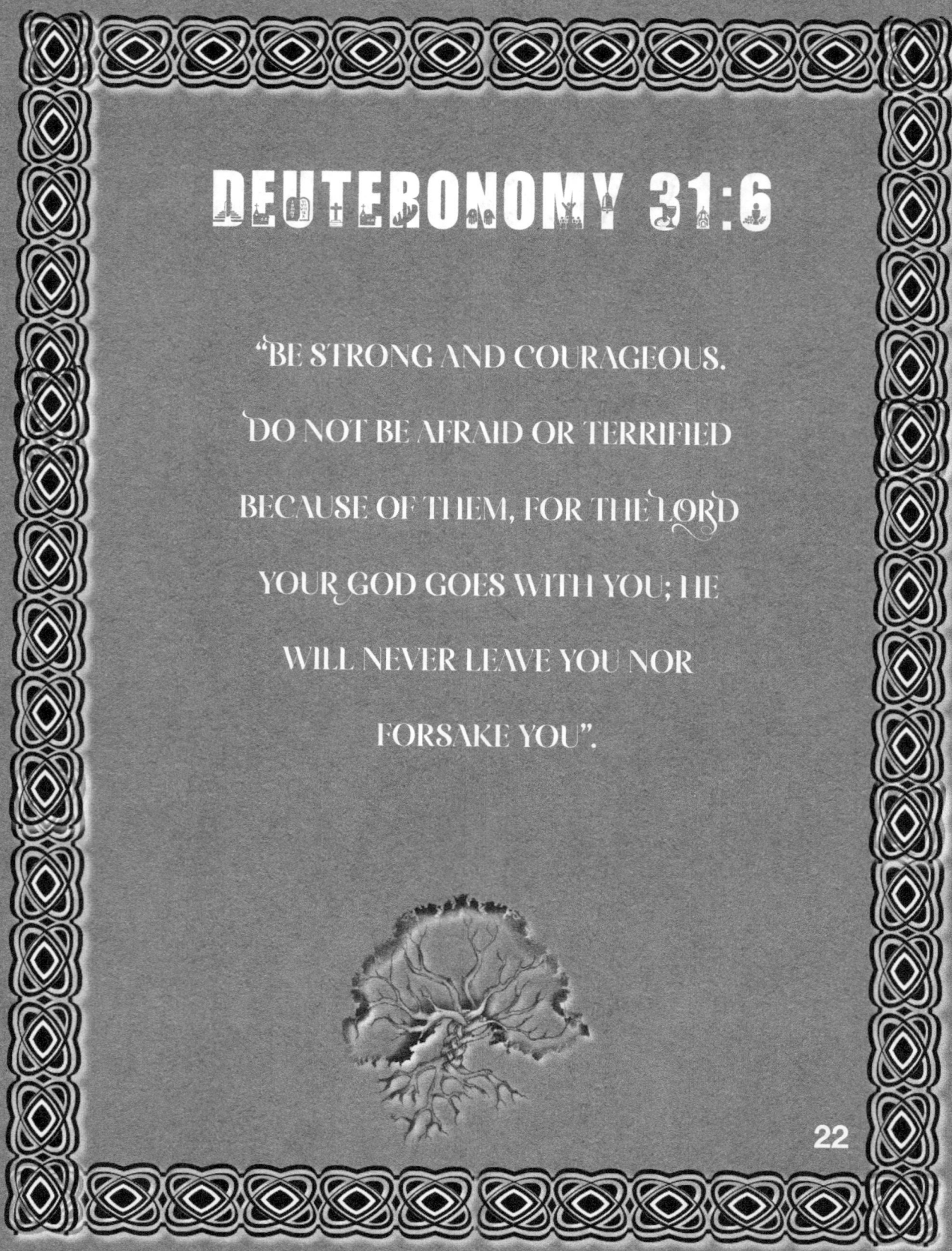

Thank You Lord

Teach Me

Guide Me

 # Reflect

Colossians 4:6

"Let your conversation be always full of grace, seasoned with salt, so that you may know how to answer everyone."

How do you respond to someone who asks you about your faith? How do you share the Word of God?

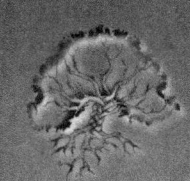
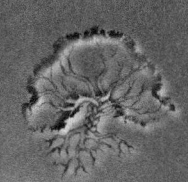

Future Generations

Highlights

My Prayers

PSALM 59:16

"I WILL SING OF YOUR STRENGTH, IN THE

MORNING I WILL SING OF YOUR LOVE;

FOR YOU ARE MY FORTRESS, MY REFUGE

IN TIMES OF TROUBLE".

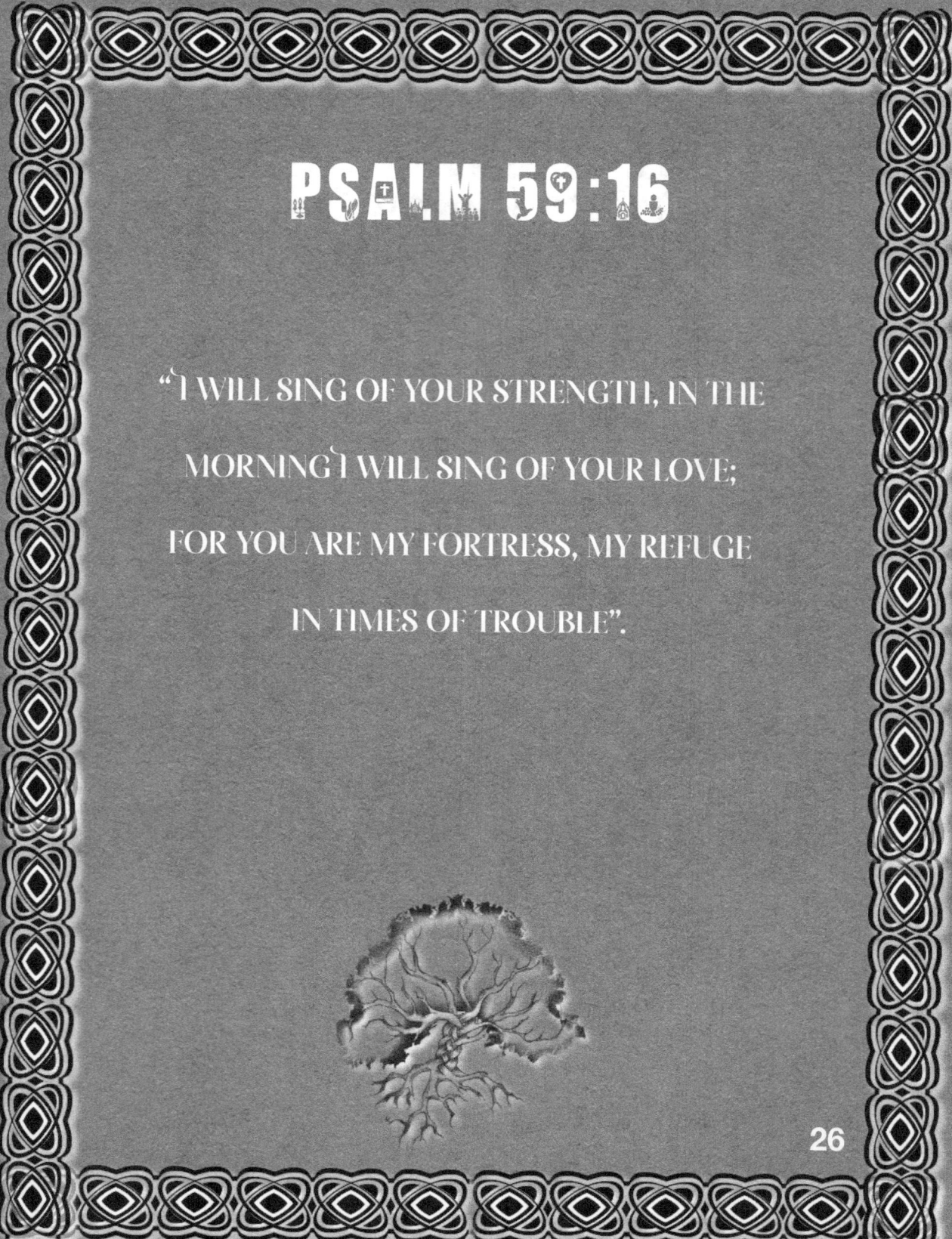

Thank You Lord

Week of: _____

♡ Teach Me ♡

_____
_____
_____
_____
_____
_____
_____
_____
_____
_____
_____

♡ Guide Me ♡

_____
_____
_____
_____
_____
_____
_____
_____
_____

 # Reflect

> ### Jeremiah 29:11
>
> "For I know the plans I have for you," declares the Lord, "plans to prosper you and not to harm you, plans to give you hope and a future"
>
> **Write about your future plans and goals. How are your plans lifted up and supported by your faith?**

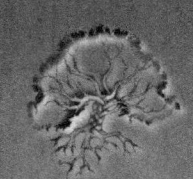

Future Generations

Highlights

My Prayers

ISAIAH 41:10

" FEAR NOT, FOR I AM WITH YOU; BE NOT

DISMAYED, FOR I AM YOUR GOD; I WILL

STRENGTHEN YOU, I WILL HELP YOU, I

WILL UPHOLD YOU WITH MY RIGHTEOUS

RIGHT HAND".

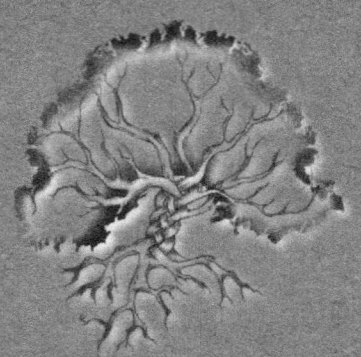

Thank You Lord

 # Teach Me

 # Guide Me

 # Reflect

Job 8:7
"Your beginnings will seem humble, so prosperous will your future be"

Think about something that was challenging for you at first but through hard work and faith, you have improved your skills?

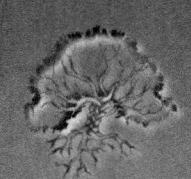

Future Generations

Highlights

My Prayers

JOHN 16:24

".UNTIL NOW YOU HAVE NOT ASKED FOR ANYTHING IN MY NAME. ASK AND YOU WILL RECEIVE, AND YOUR JOY WILL BE COMPLETE".

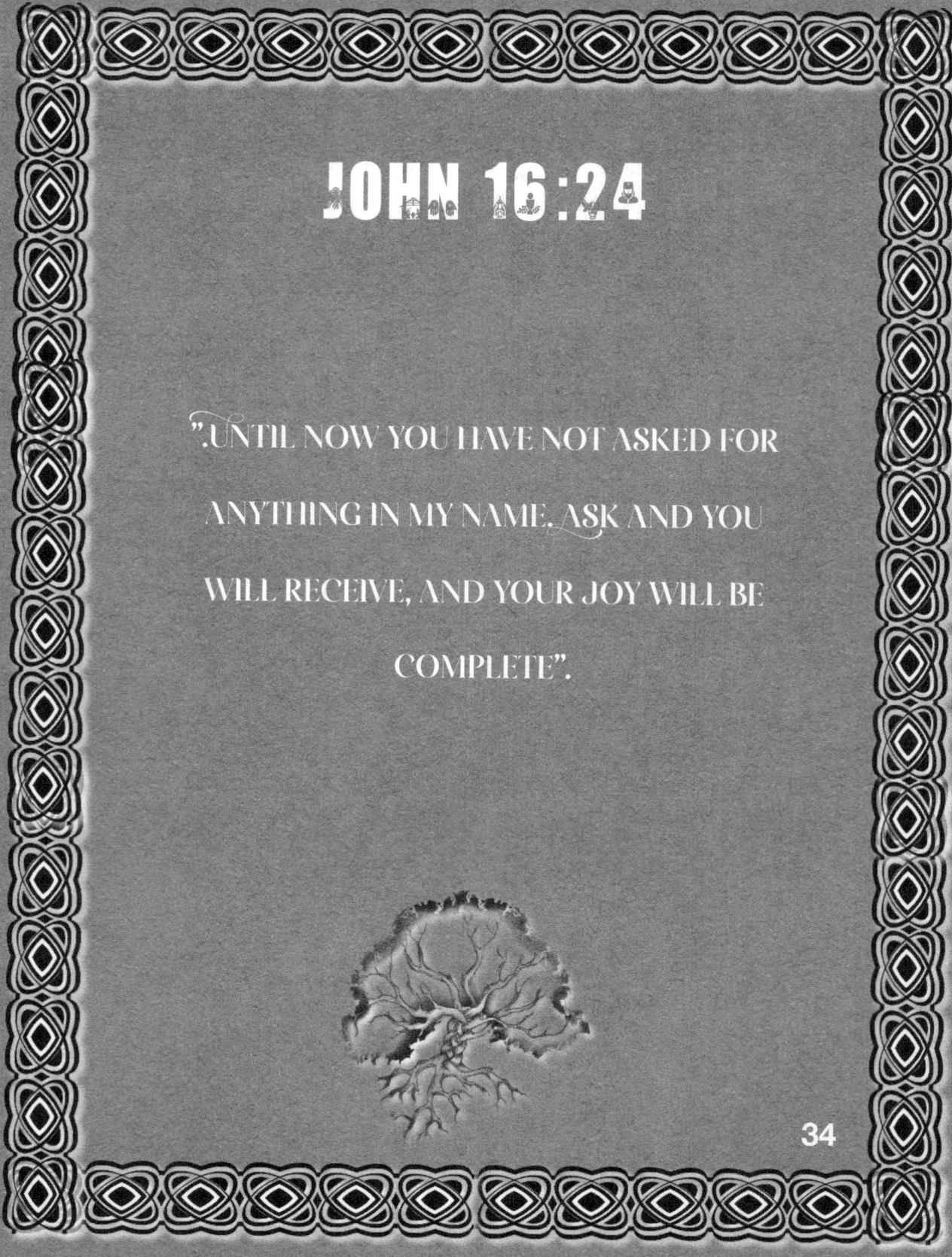

Thank You Lord

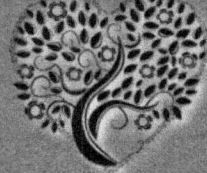

Teach Me

Guide Me

 # Reflect

1 John 4:7
"Dear friends, let us love one another, for love comes from God. Everyone who loves has been born of God and knows God."

Write about ways you show love and kindness in your everyday life. Reflect on ways you see love in the world

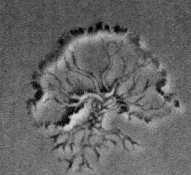
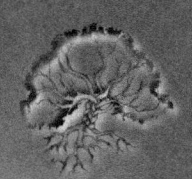

Future Generations

Highlights

My Prayers

ROMANS 15:4

" FOR EVERYTHING THAT WAS WRITTEN IN THE PAST WAS WRITTEN TO TEACH US, SO THAT THROUGH THE ENDURANCE TAUGHT IN THE SCRIPTURES AND THE ENCOURAGEMENT THEY PROVIDE WE MIGHT HAVE HOPE."

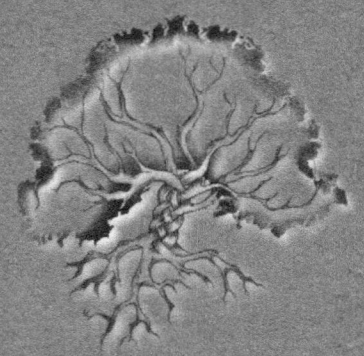

Thank You Lord

Week of: _____

Teach Me

Guide Me

 # Reflect

Matthew 6:25-26

"Therefore I tell you, do not worry about your life, what you will eat or drink; or about your body, what you will wear. Is not life more than food, and the body more than clothes? Look at the birds of the air; they do not sow or reap or store away in barns, and yet your heavenly Father feeds them. Are you not much more valuable than they?"

Think about some things you are worried about. Write them down, and then let them go to God.

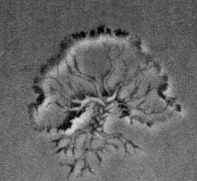
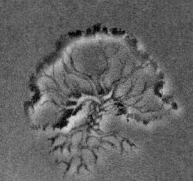

Future Generations

Highlights

My Prayers

JOSHUA 1:9

"HAVE I NOT COMMANDED YOU? BE STRONG AND COURAGEOUS. DO NOT BE FRIGHTENED, AND DO NOT BE DISMAYED, FOR THE LORD YOUR GOD IS WITH YOU WHEREVER YOU GO.".

Thank You Lord

Week of: _____

🖤 Teach Me 🖤

_____
_____
_____
_____
_____
_____
_____
_____
_____
_____

🖤 Guide Me 🖤

_____
_____
_____
_____
_____
_____
_____
_____
_____

 # Reflect

1 Timothy 4:12

"Don't let anyone look down on you because you are young, but set an example

for the believers in speech, in conduct, in love, in faith and in purity"

How can you overcome stereotypes people hold about young people?

Future Generations

Highlights

My Prayers

1 PETER 5:7

"CAST ALL YOUR ANXIETY ON HIM

BECAUSE HE CARES FOR YOU."

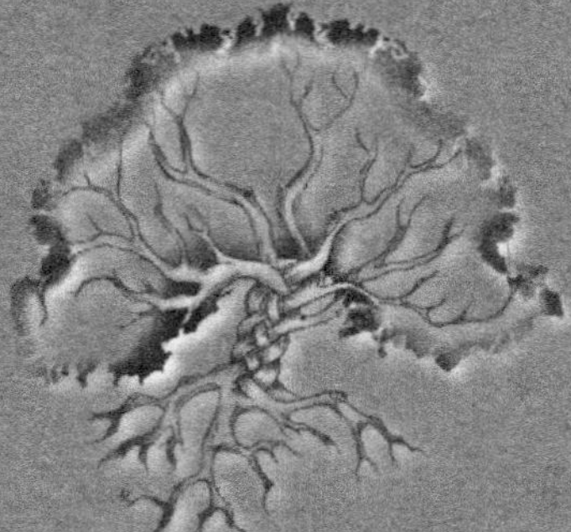

Thank You Lord

Week of: _____

🖤 Teach Me 🖤

_____
_____
_____
_____
_____
_____
_____
_____
_____
_____

🖤 Guide Me 🖤

_____
_____
_____
_____
_____
_____
_____
_____

 # Reflect

Matthew 19:26

"With God all things are possible".

What does this verse mean to you?

_____

_____

_____

_____

_____

_____

_____

_____

_____

_____

_____

_____

_____

_____

_____

_____

_____

_____

_____

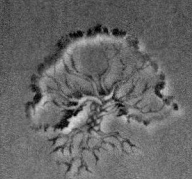
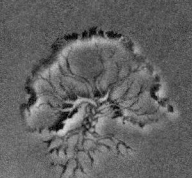

Future Generations

Highlights

My Prayers

COLOSSIANS 3:15

"LET THE PEACE OF CHRIST RULE IN YOUR HEARTS, SINCE AS MEMBERS OF ONE BODY YOU WERE CALLED TO PEACE, AND BE THANKFUL".

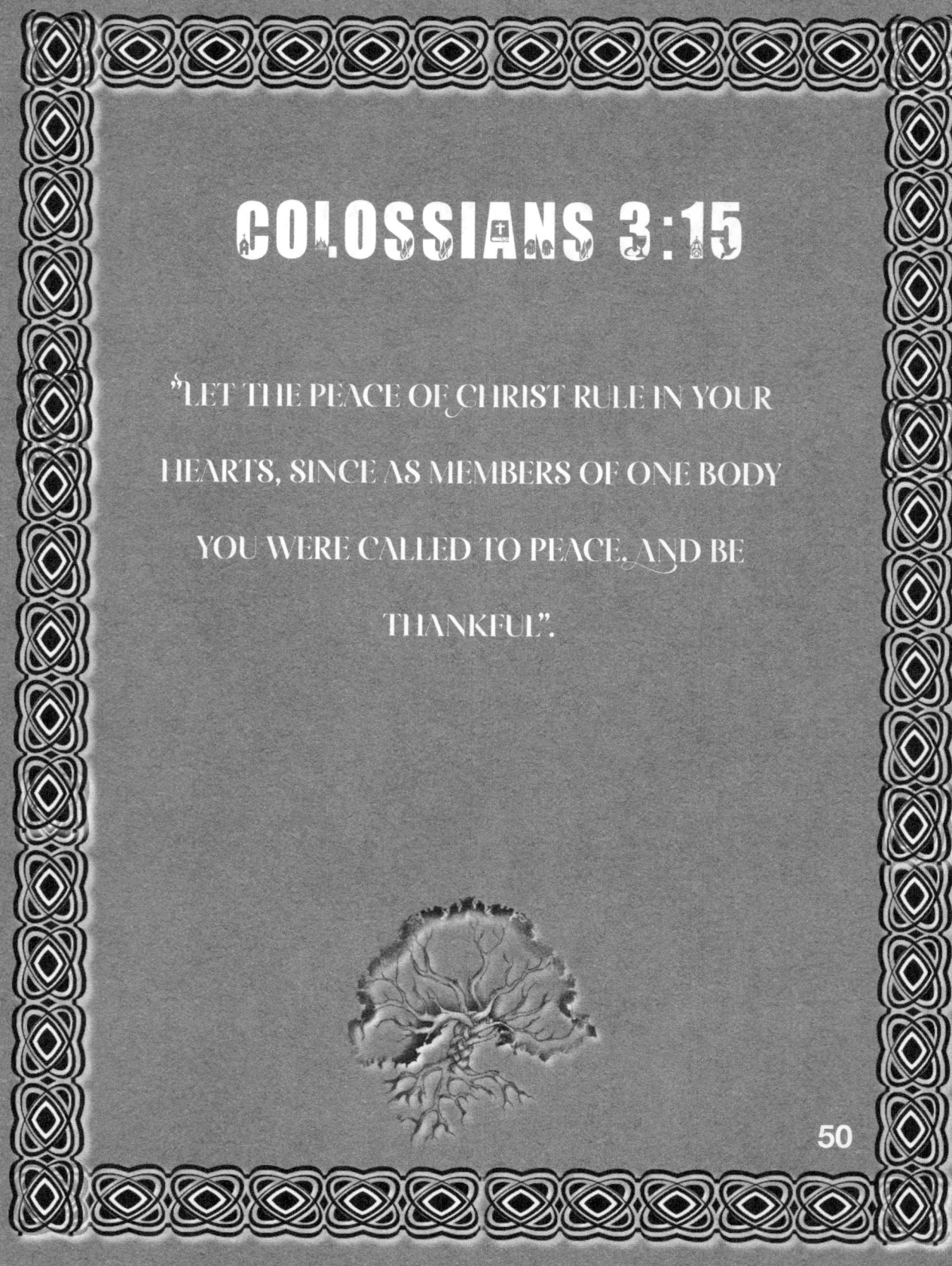

Thank You Lord

Week of: _____

Teach Me

Guide Me

 # Reflect

Scripture says faith is a gift. How are you sure that you have

accepted that gift?

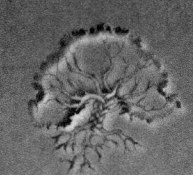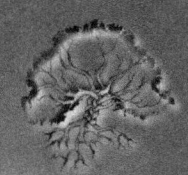

Future Generations

Highlights

My Prayers

ROMANS 10:9

"IF YOU DECLARE WITH YOUR MOUTH,

"JESUS IS LORD," AND BELIEVE IN YOUR

HEART THAT GOD RAISED HIM FROM

THE DEAD, YOU WILL BE SAVED.".

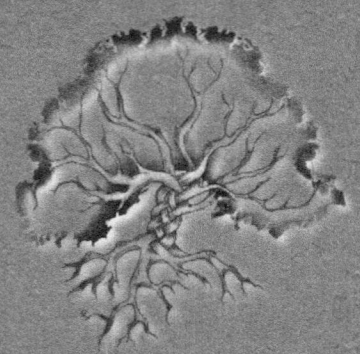

Thank You Lord

Week of: _____

 ## Teach Me

_____
_____
_____
_____
_____
_____
_____
_____
_____

 ## Guide Me

_____
_____
_____
_____
_____
_____
_____
_____

 # Reflect

Have you ever heard God's voice and was disobedient? What were the consequences? How was your faith strengthened or weakened as a result?

_____

_____

_____

_____

_____

_____

_____

_____

_____

_____

_____

_____

_____

_____

_____

_____

_____

_____

_____

_____

_____

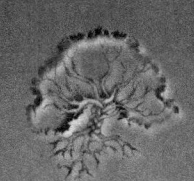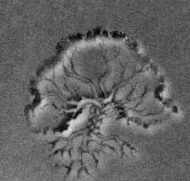

Future Generations

Highlights

My Prayers

HEBREWS 11:6

"WITHOUT FAITH IT IS IMPOSSIBLE TO

PLEASE GOD, BECAUSE ANYONE WHO

COMES TO HIM MUST BELIEVE THAT HE

EXISTS AND THAT HE REWARDS THOSE

WHO EARNESTLY SEEK HIM".

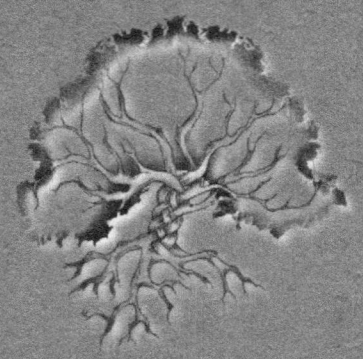

Thank You Lord

Week of: _____

 # Teach Me

_____
_____
_____
_____
_____
_____
_____
_____
_____
_____

 # Guide Me

_____
_____
_____
_____
_____
_____
_____
_____
_____

 # Reflect

If the Bible were to be rewritten with you as a character

in it, what would you want to be remembered for?

_____

_____

_____

_____

_____

_____

_____

_____

_____

_____

_____

_____

_____

_____

_____

_____

_____

_____

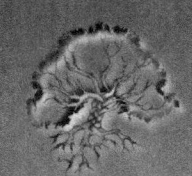

Future Generations

Highlights

My Prayers

2 CORINTHIANS 4:18

"SO WE FIX OUR EYES NOT ON WHAT IS SEEN, BUT ON WHAT IS UNSEEN, SINCE WHAT IS SEEN IS TEMPORARY, BUT WHAT IS UNSEEN IS ETERNAL".

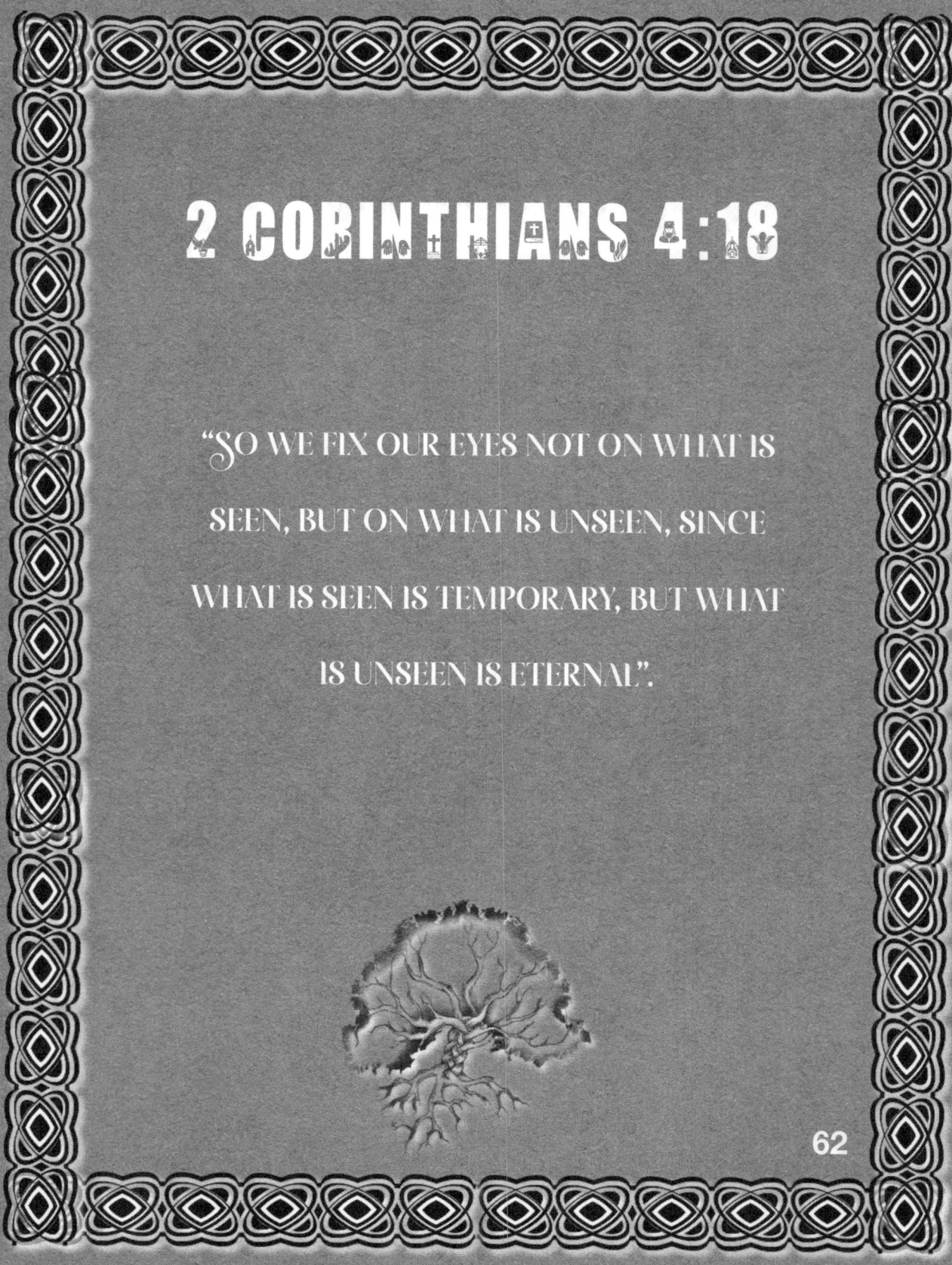

Thank You Lord

Week of: _____

 # Teach Me

 # Guide Me

 # Reflect

How has your faith grown over the years? Can you identify specific events that caused your faith to grow? How has your faith changed over the years? And how have you changed as a result of this?

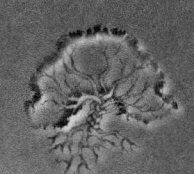

Future Generations

Highlights

My Prayers

ROMANS 15:4

"FOR EVERYTHING THAT WAS WRITTEN IN THE PAST WAS WRITTEN TO TEACH US, SO THAT THROUGH THE ENDURANCE TAUGHT IN THE SCRIPTURES AND THE ENCOURAGEMENT THEY PROVIDE WE MIGHT HAVE HOPE".

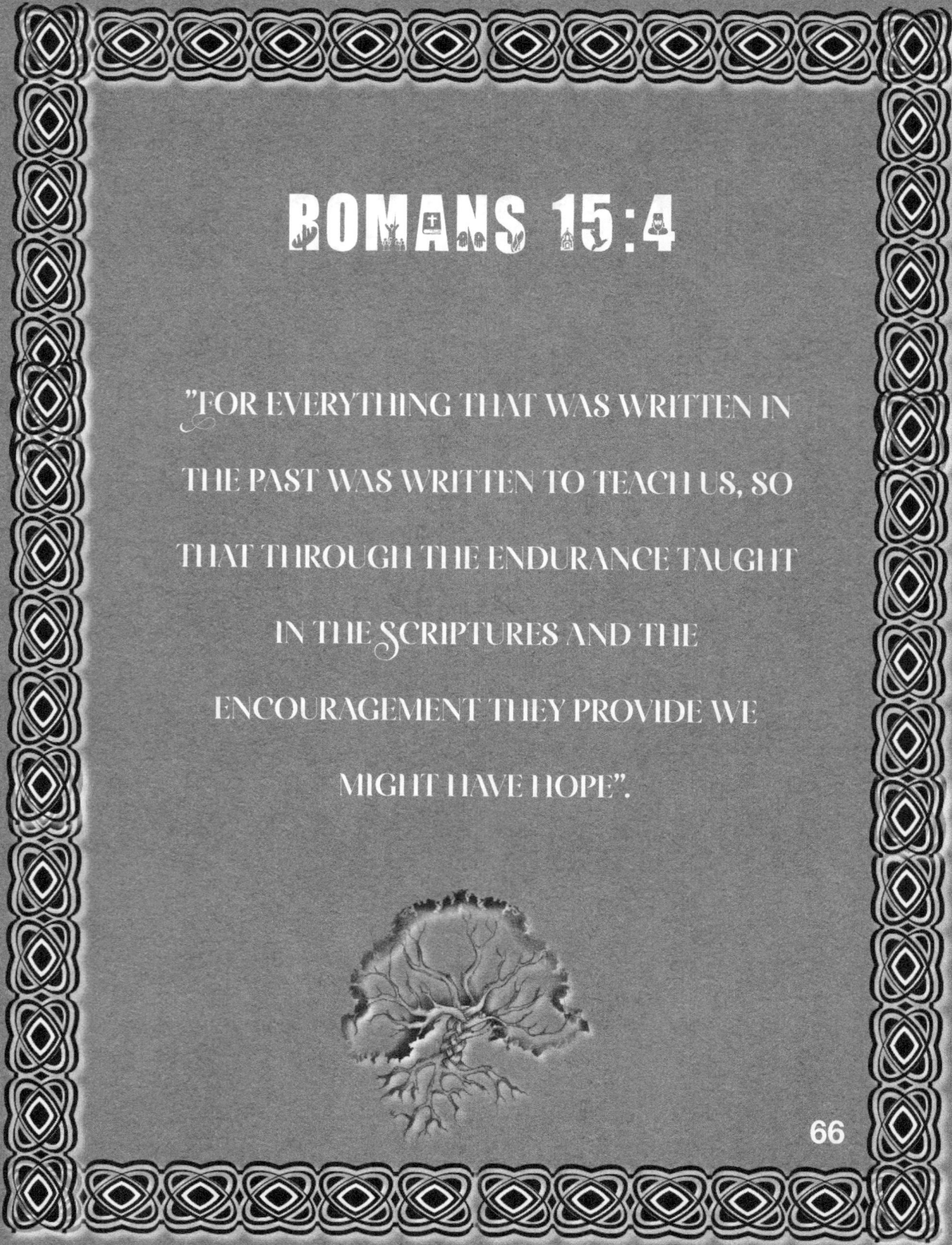

Thank You Lord

Week of: _____

 # Teach Me

_____
_____
_____
_____
_____
_____
_____
_____
_____
_____
_____

 # Guide Me

_____
_____
_____
_____
_____
_____
_____
_____
_____
_____

 # Reflect

What is your favorite scripture passage is and

why?

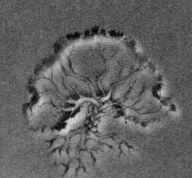

Future Generations

Highlights

My Prayers

PROVERBS 3:5-6

"TRUST IN THE LORD WITH ALL YOUR HEART AND LEAN NOT ON YOUR OWN UNDERSTANDING"

".

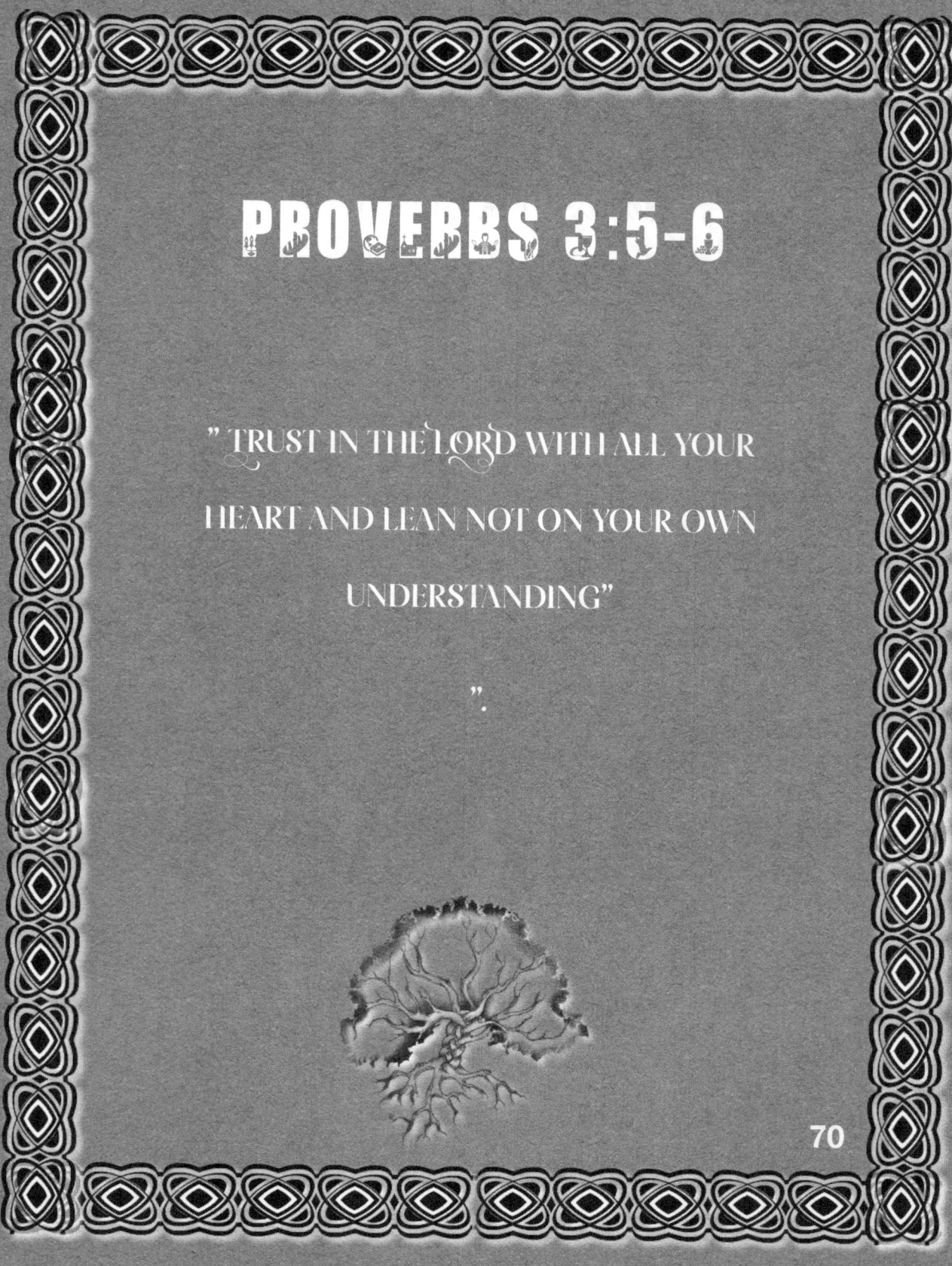

Thank You Lord

Week of: _____

♥ Teach Me ♥

_____
_____
_____
_____
_____
_____
_____
_____

♥ Guide Me ♥

_____
_____
_____
_____
_____
_____
_____
_____

 # Reflect

List all the things you believe about God. Pick

one to be your mantra for week

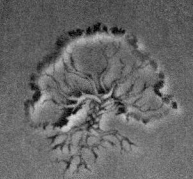

Future Generations

Highlights

My Prayers

ISAIAH 12:2

"GOD IS MY SALVATION; I WILL TRUST AND

NOT BE AFRAID. THE LORD, THE LORD

HIMSELF, IS MY STRENGTH AND MY DEFENSE;

HE HAS BECOME MY SALVATION"

"

Thank You Lord

Week of: _____

 Teach Me

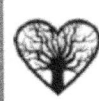 Guide Me

 # Reflect

God is in the business of changing hearts. I pray

that God changes the heart of?

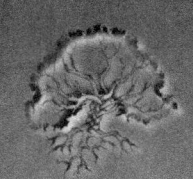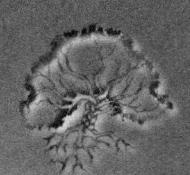

Future Generations

Highlights

My Prayers

EPHESIANS 4:32

"BE KIND AND COMPASSIONATE TO ONE ANOTHER, FORGIVING EACH OTHER, JUST AS IN CHRIST GOD FORGAVE YOU".

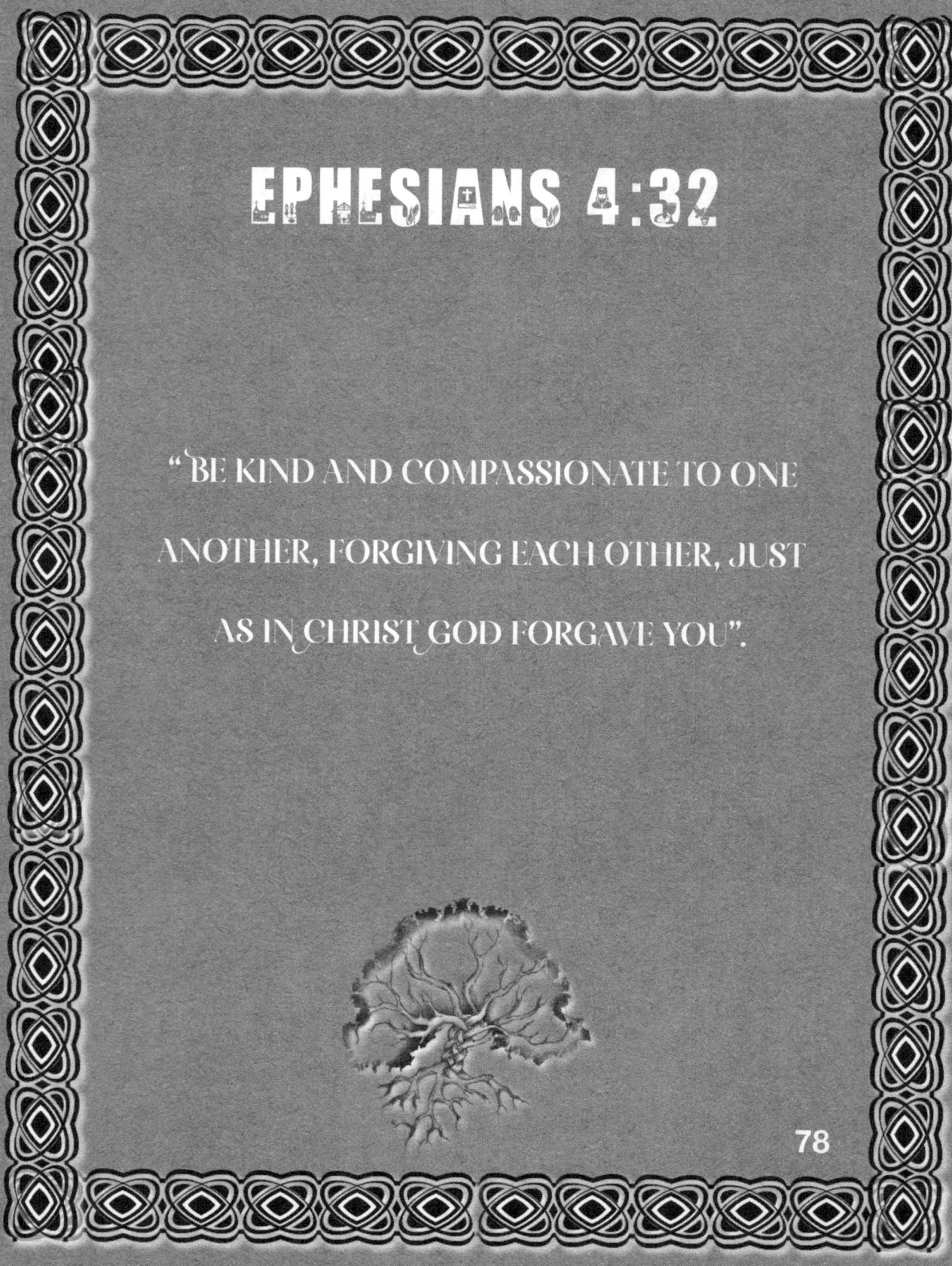

Thank You Lord

Week of: _____

 # Teach Me

_____
_____
_____
_____
_____
_____
_____
_____
_____
_____
_____

 # Guide Me

_____
_____
_____
_____
_____
_____
_____
_____
_____

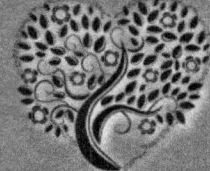

 # Reflect

This week resolve to forgive. Write a letter to someone you need to forgive offering forgiveness to them

_____
_____
_____
_____
_____
_____
_____
_____
_____
_____
_____
_____
_____
_____
_____
_____
_____
_____
_____
_____

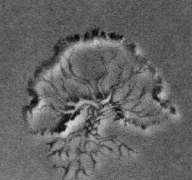

Future Generations

Highlights

My Prayers

EPHESIANS 6:14

"STAND FIRM THEN, WITH THE BELT OF

TRUTH BUCKLED AROUND YOUR

WAIST, WITH THE BREASTPLATE OF

RIGHTEOUSNESS IN PLACE".

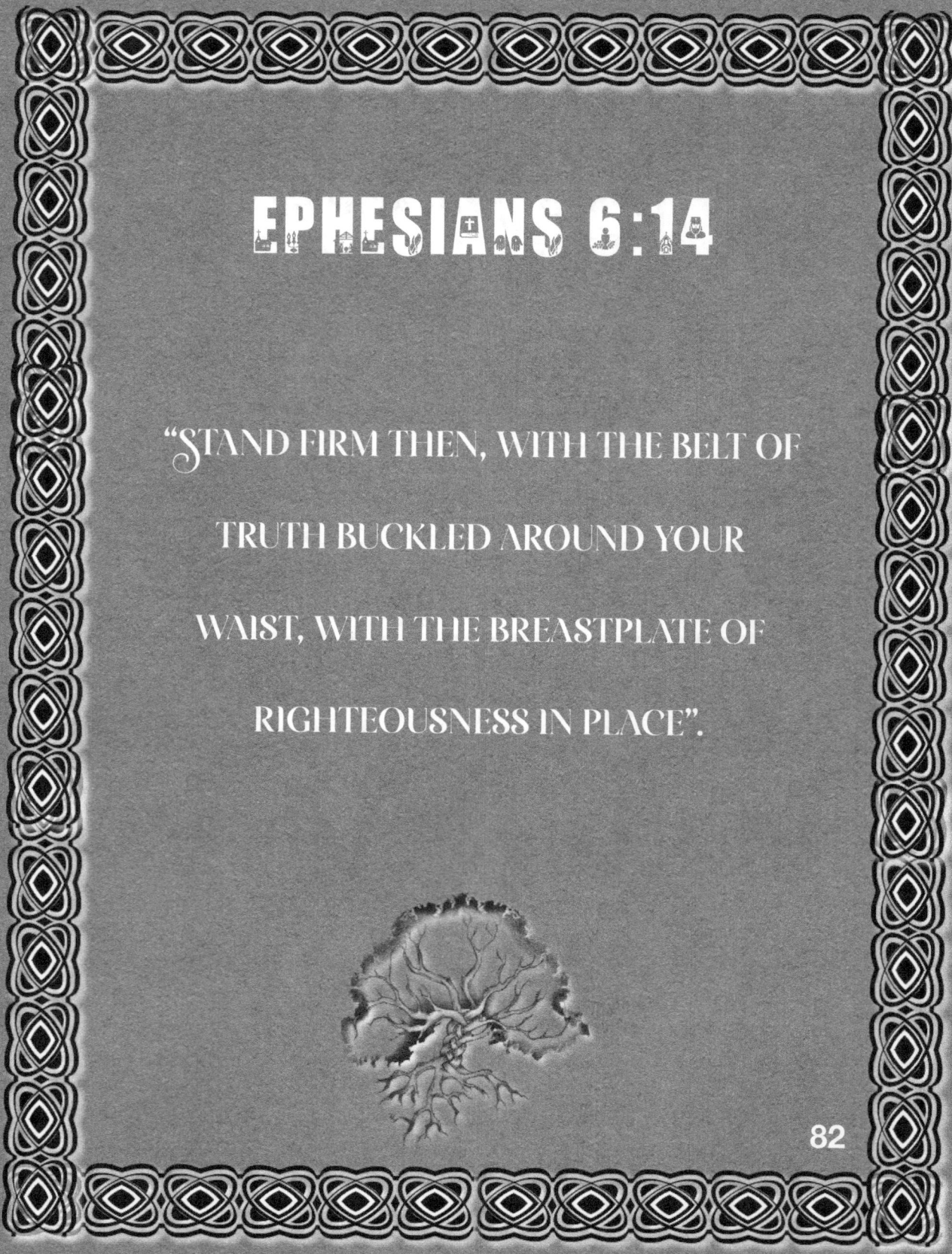

Thank You Lord

Week of: _____

 Teach Me

_____
_____
_____
_____
_____
_____
_____
_____
_____
_____

 Guide Me

_____
_____
_____
_____
_____
_____
_____
_____

 # Reflect

What things in nature can you use to prompt your

faith? Why have you chosen this symbol?

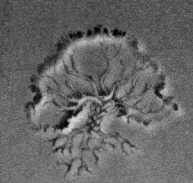
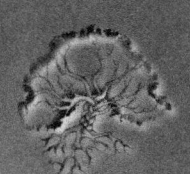

Future Generations

Highlights

My Prayers

PROVERBS 12:17

"HE THAT SPEAKETH TRUTH

SHEWETH FORTH

RIGHTEOUSNESS: BUT A FALSE

WITNESS DECEIT"

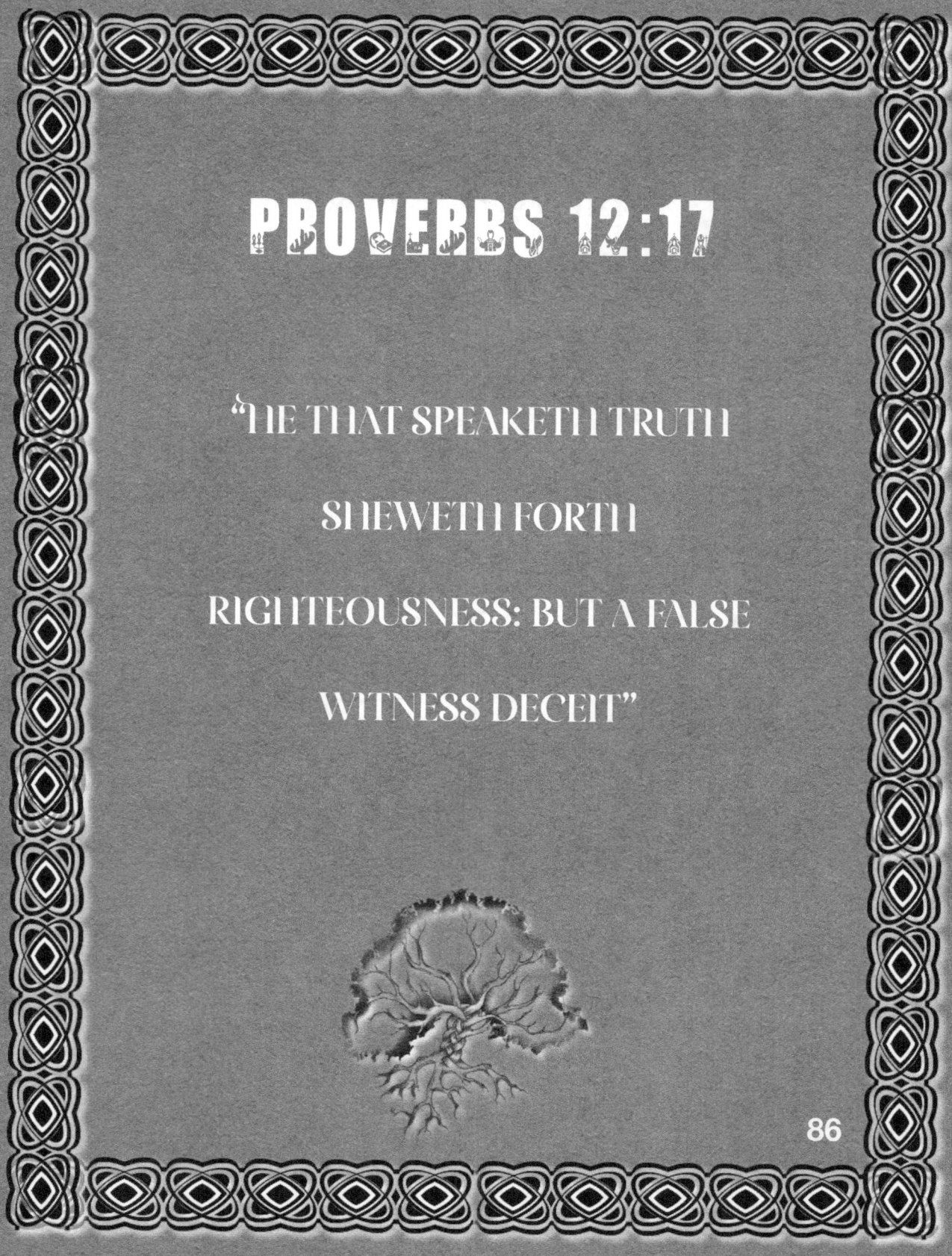

Thank You Lord

Week of: _____

 # Teach Me

_____
_____
_____
_____
_____
_____
_____
_____
_____
_____
_____
_____

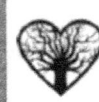 # Guide Me

_____
_____
_____
_____
_____
_____
_____
_____
_____
_____
_____

 # Reflect

What do you see when you pray? How do you imagine

God? Write a vivid picture of what you think God looks

or feel like. Where are you? What do you smell, feel,

taste, see?

_____
_____
_____
_____
_____
_____
_____
_____
_____
_____
_____
_____
_____
_____
_____
_____
_____
_____
_____

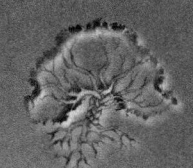

Future Generations

Highlights

My Prayers

EPHESIANS 5:2

"WALK IN THE WAY OF LOVE, JUST AS CHRIST LOVED US AND GAVE HIMSELF UP FOR US AS A FRAGRANT OFFERING AND SACRIFICE TO GOD".

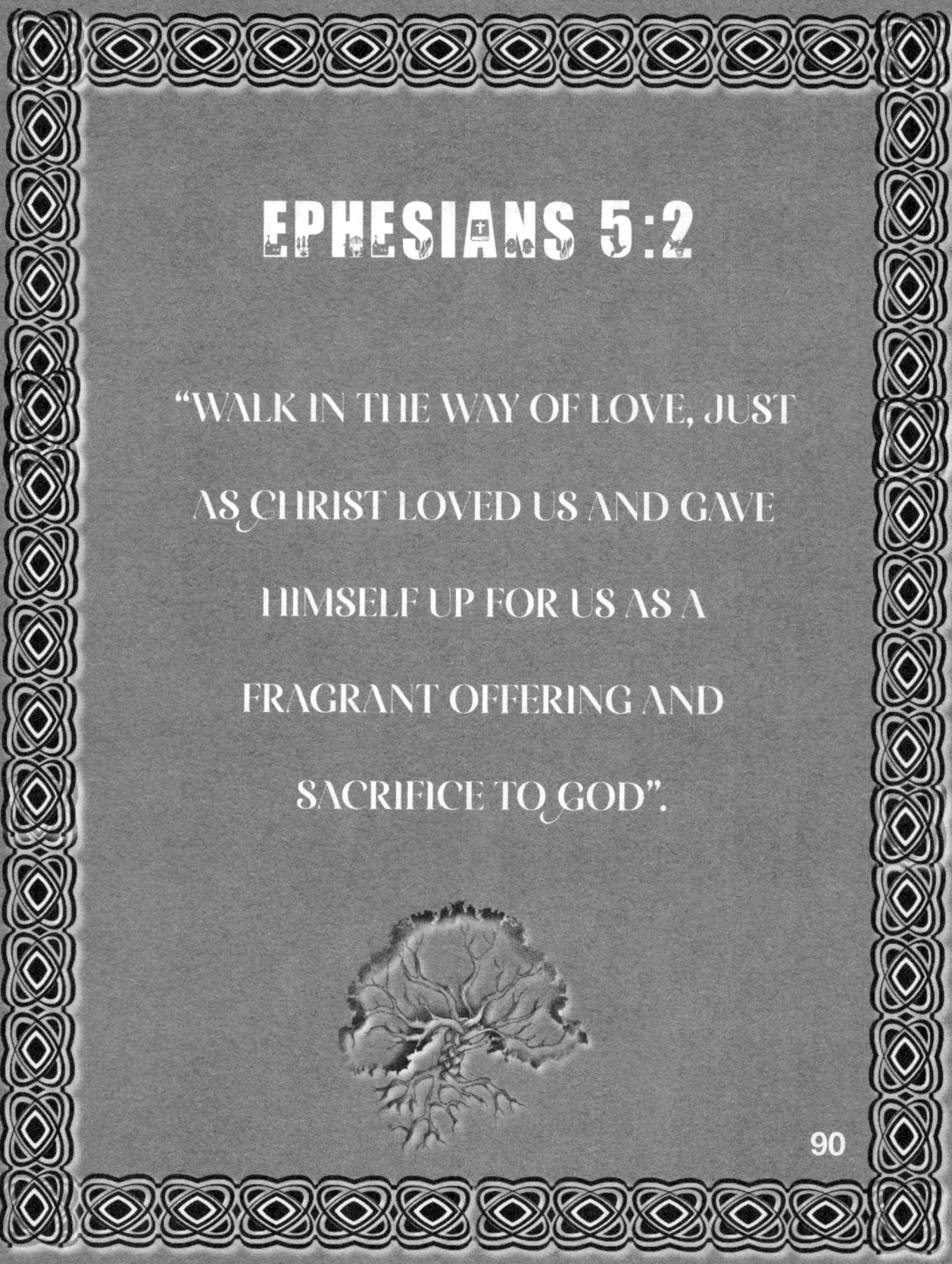

Thank You Lord

Week of: _____

 Teach Me

_____
_____
_____
_____
_____
_____
_____
_____
_____

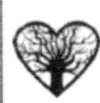 **Guide Me**

_____
_____
_____
_____
_____
_____
_____
_____

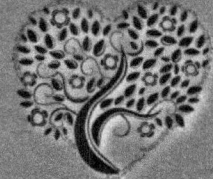

 # Reflect

Which book in the Bible do you go when you're

struggling in faith? Why?

_____

_____

_____

_____

_____

_____

_____

_____

_____

_____

_____

_____

_____

_____

_____

_____

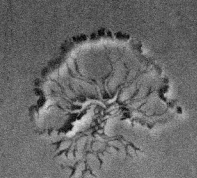
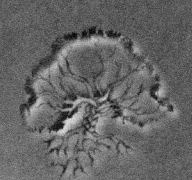

Future Generations

Highlights

My Prayers

COLOSSIANS 3:15

"LET THE PEACE OF CHRIST RULE IN YOUR HEARTS, TO WHICH INDEED YOU WERE CALLED IN ONE BODY, AND BE THANKFUL".

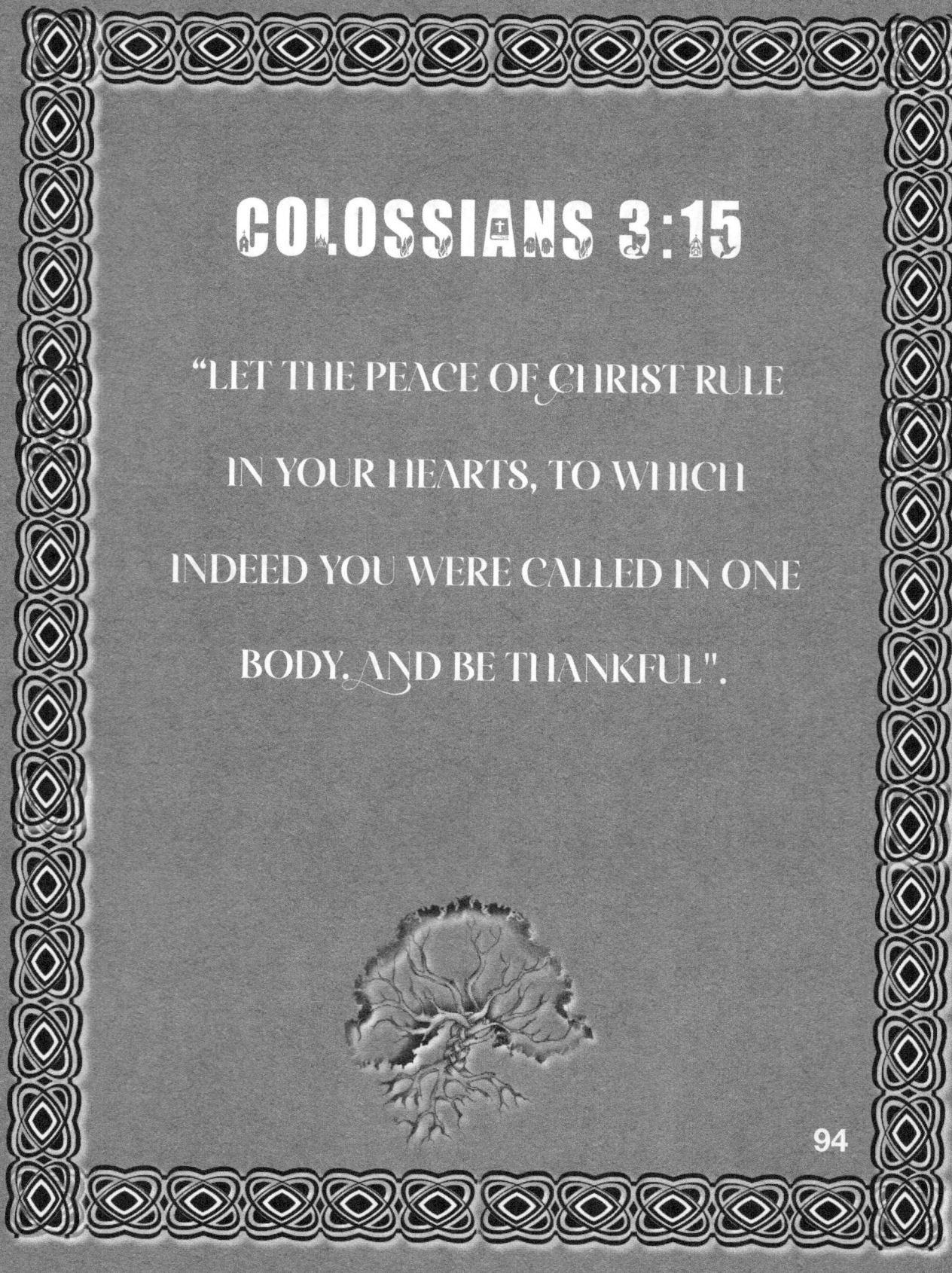

Thank You Lord

Week of: _____

 # Teach Me

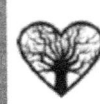 # Guide Me

 # Reflect

With God all things are possible. What things are

possible for you with God by your side?

_____
_____
_____
_____
_____
_____
_____
_____
_____
_____
_____
_____
_____
_____
_____
_____
_____
_____
_____
_____

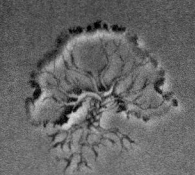
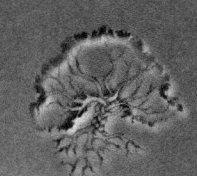

Future Generations

Highlights

My Prayers

PSALM 138

"A PSALM, FOR GIVING GRATEFUL PRAISE. SHOUT FOR JOY TO THE LORD, ALL THE EARTH".

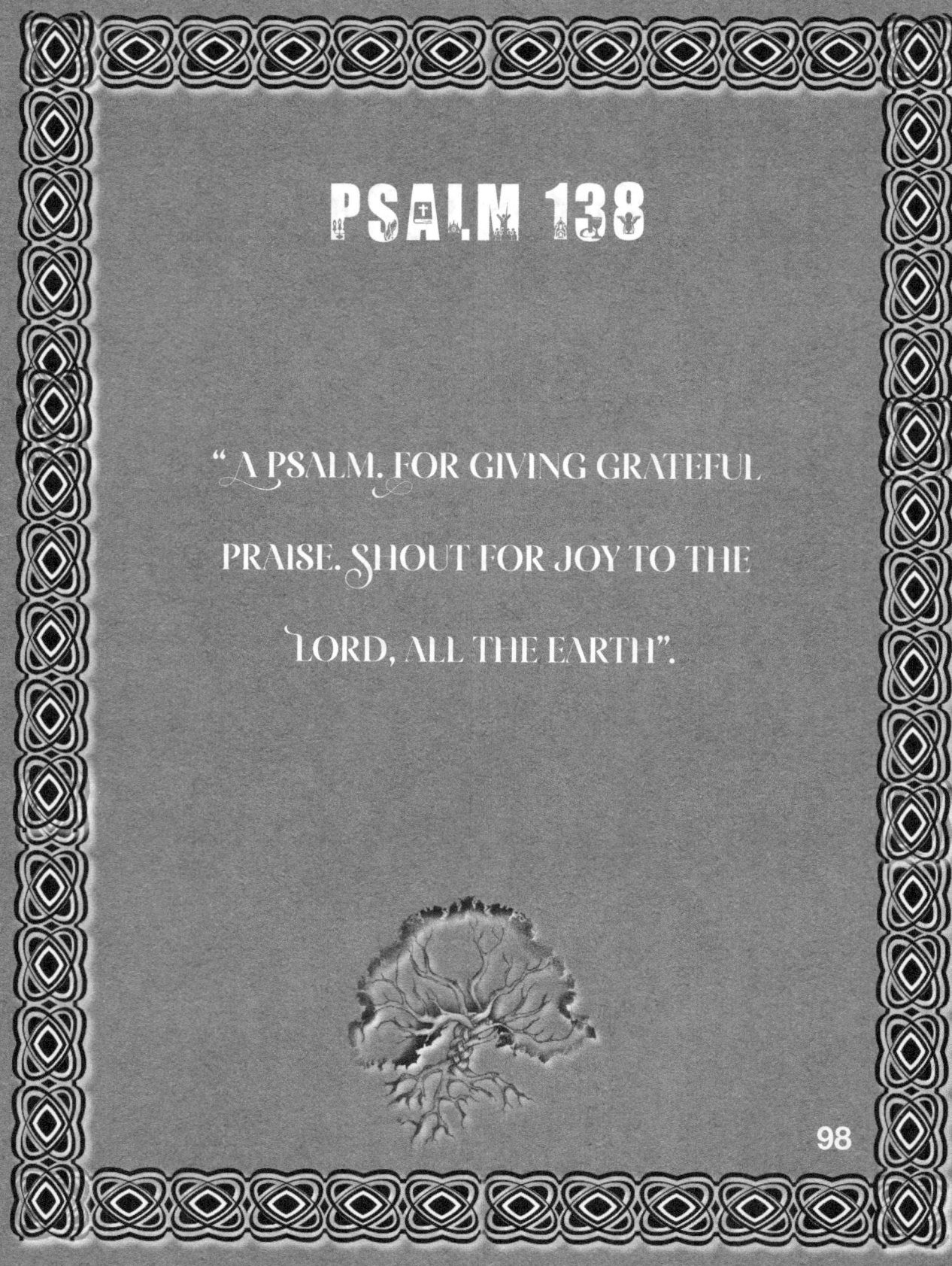

Thank You Lord

Week of: _____

 # Teach Me

_____
_____
_____
_____
_____
_____
_____
_____
_____
_____

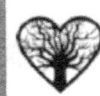 # Guide Me

_____
_____
_____
_____
_____
_____
_____
_____

 # Reflect

When you think of faith, what non-Bible quote comes to mind? Why does it hold such significance for you?

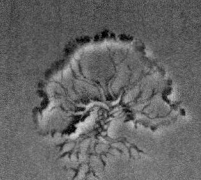
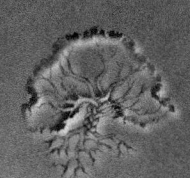

Future Generations

Highlights

My Prayers

ECCLESIASTES 5:10

"WHOEVER LOVES MONEY NEVER HAS ENOUGH; WHOEVER LOVES WEALTH IS NEVER SATISFIED WITH THEIR INCOME. THIS TOO IS MEANINGLESS.".

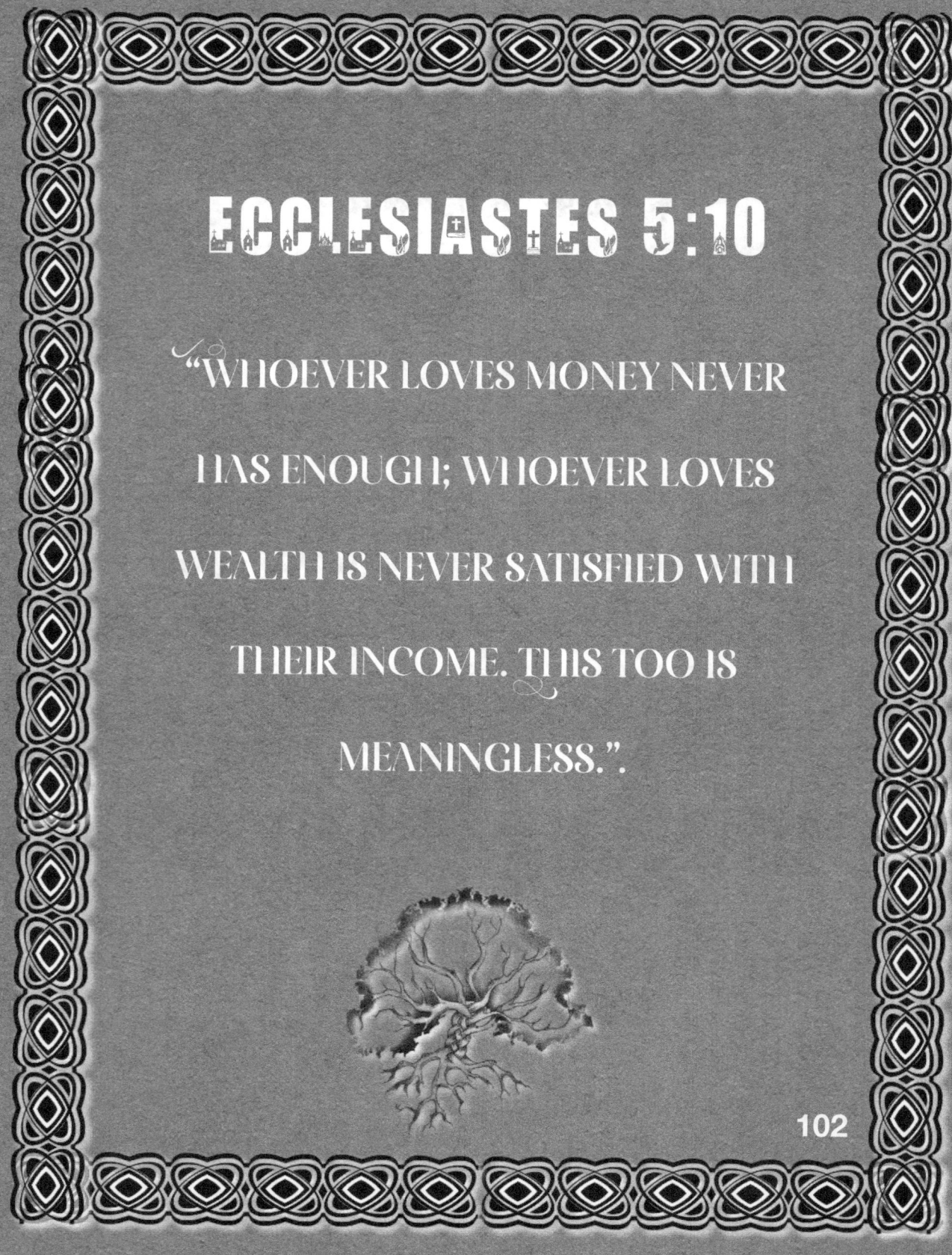

Thank You Lord

 # Teach Me

 # Guide Me

 # Reflect

What is the connection between faith and

purpose?

_____

_____

_____

_____

_____

_____

_____

_____

_____

_____

_____

_____

_____

_____

_____

_____

_____

_____

_____

_____

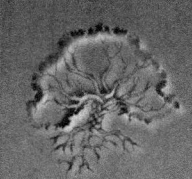

Future Generations

Highlights

My Prayers

HEBREWS 13:5

"KEEP YOUR LIVES FREE FROM THE

LOVE OF MONEY AND BE CONTENT

WITH WHAT YOU HAVE, BECAUSE

GOD HAS SAID, "NEVER WILL I LEAVE

YOU; NEVER WILL I FORSAKE YOU.".

Thank You Lord

Week of: _____

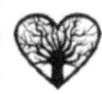 **Teach Me**

_____
_____
_____
_____
_____
_____
_____
_____
_____

 **Guide Me**

_____
_____
_____
_____
_____
_____
_____
_____

 # Reflect

When you think of fear and doubt, which Bible character comes to mind? How did they overcome it? What can you learn from them?

_____
_____
_____
_____
_____
_____
_____
_____
_____
_____
_____
_____
_____
_____
_____
_____
_____
_____
_____
_____
_____

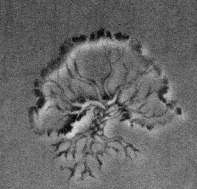
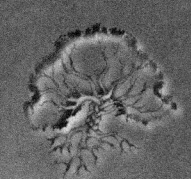

Future Generations

Highlights

My Prayers

ECCLESIASTES 5:15

"EVERYONE COMES NAKED FROM

THEIR MOTHER'S WOMB, AND AS

EVERYONE COMES, SO THEY DEPART.

THEY TAKE NOTHING FROM THEIR

TOIL THAT THEY CAN CARRY IN

THEIR HANDS".

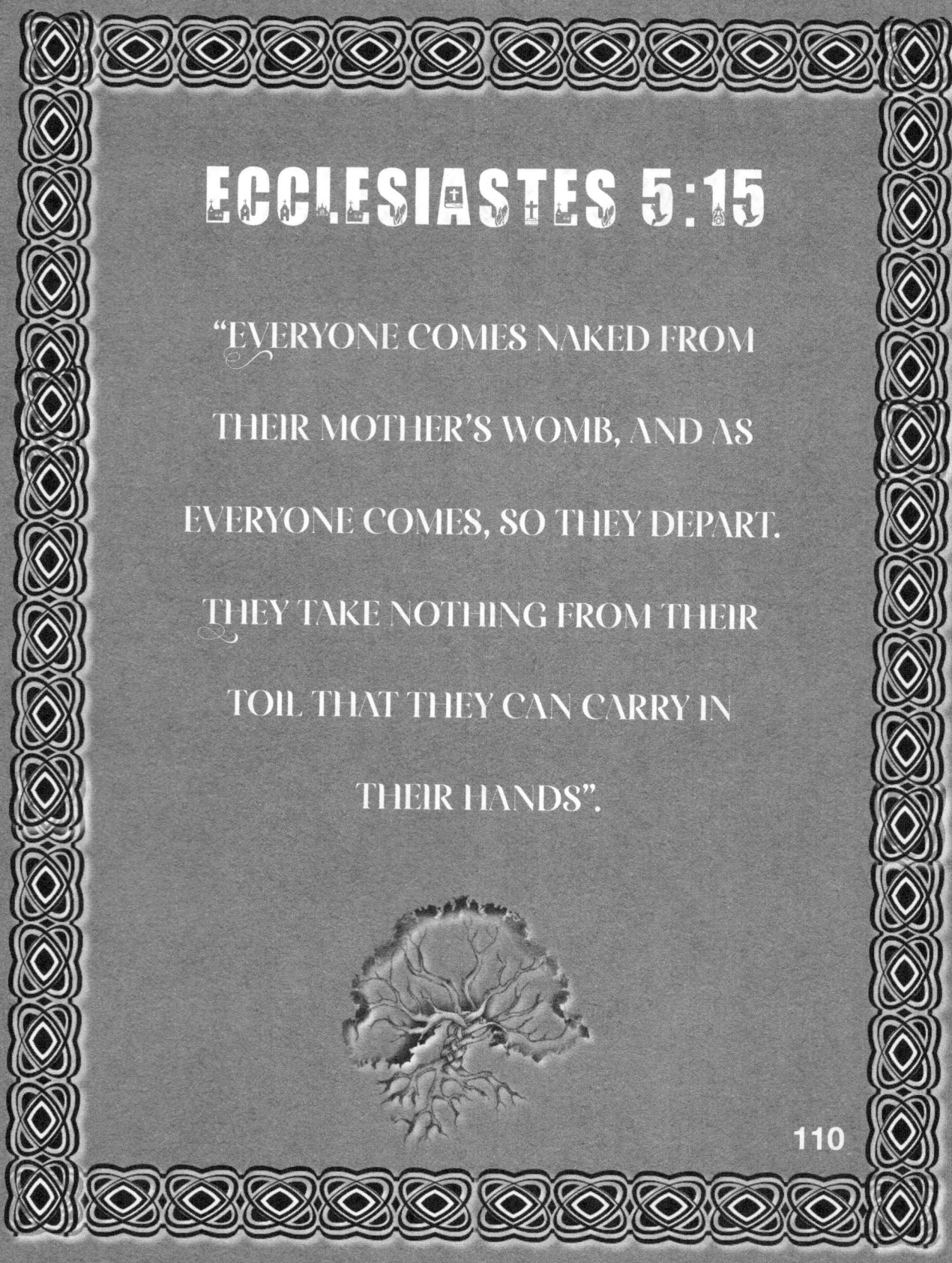

 # Reflect

Imagine you are in the crowd and Jesus is passing by. You cry out "Jesus, Son of God, have mercy on me." He stops, finds you in the crowd and say "What would you have me do?" What do you say to him?

Future Generations

Highlights

My Prayers

PSALMS 146:8

"THE LORD GIVES SIGHT TO THE BLIND, THE LORD LIFTS UP THOSE WHO ARE BOWED DOWN, THE LORD LOVES THE RIGHTEOUS".

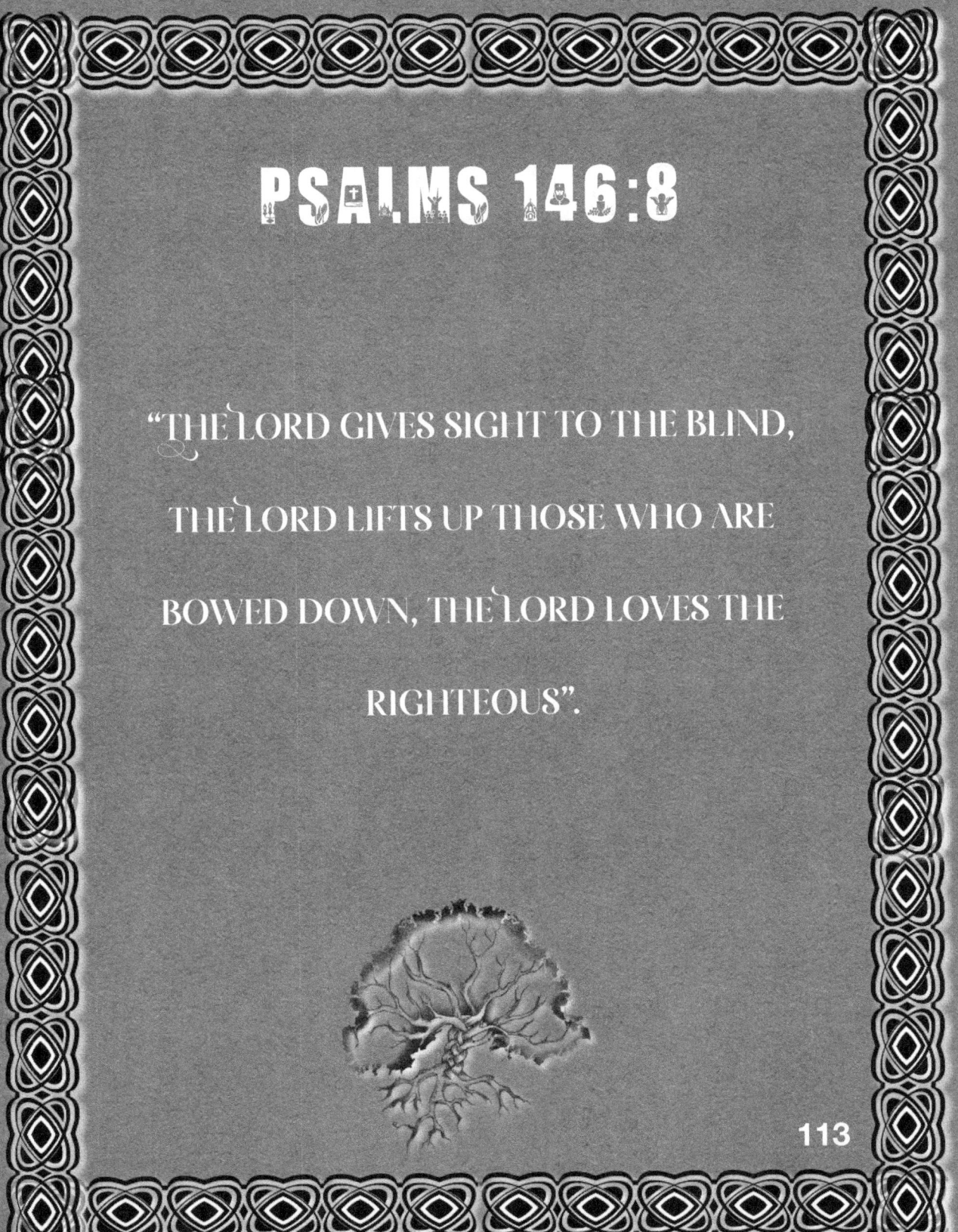

Thank You Lord

Week of: _____

 Teach Me

_____
_____
_____
_____
_____
_____
_____
_____
_____
_____

 Guide Me

_____
_____
_____
_____
_____
_____
_____
_____
_____

 # Reflect

What is imposter syndrome? Can you identify a Bible character who struggled with it? How did they conquer it? What Biblical truth contradicts that lie?

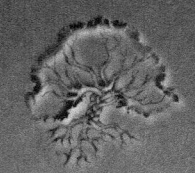
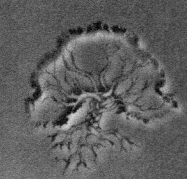

Future Generations

Highlights

My Prayers

ISAIAH 41:10

"SO DO NOT FEAR, FOR I AM WITH YOU; DO NOT BE DISMAYED, FOR I AM YOUR GOD. I WILL STRENGTHEN YOU AND HELP YOU; I WILL UPHOLD YOU WITH MY RIGHTEOUS RIGHT HAND".

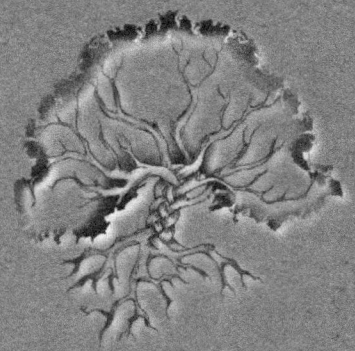

Thank You Lord

Week of: _____

 Teach Me

_____
_____
_____
_____
_____
_____
_____
_____
_____

 Guide Me

_____
_____
_____
_____
_____
_____
_____
_____

 # *Reflect*

> If you could choose *one* spiritual ideal to have right now, what
> would you want? (ie. patience, wisdom, empathy for others,
> knowing the right words to say to a friend, etc.) *Ask God for*
> *guidance.*

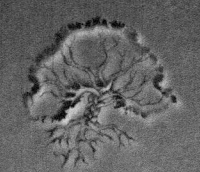
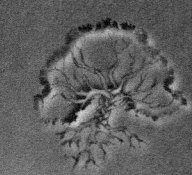

Future Generations

Highlights

My Prayers

REVELATION 21:4

"HE WILL WIPE EVERY TEAR FROM THEIR EYES. THERE WILL BE NO MORE DEATH' OR MOURNING OR CRYING OR PAIN, FOR THE OLD ORDER OF THINGS HAS PASSED AWAY".

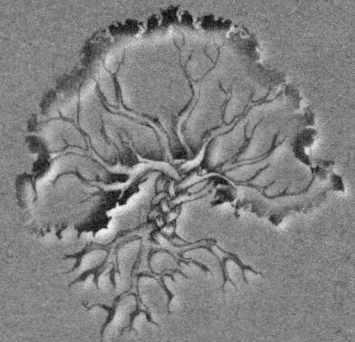

Thank You Lord

 Teach Me

_____
_____
_____
_____
_____
_____
_____
_____
_____

 Guide Me

_____
_____
_____
_____
_____
_____
_____
_____

 # *Reflect*

How are you serving God on a daily basis? It doesn't have to be something big- it could be something as simple as cleaning the house so another person doesn't have to.

_____
_____
_____
_____
_____
_____
_____
_____
_____
_____
_____
_____
_____
_____
_____
_____
_____
_____
_____
_____

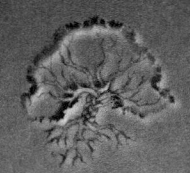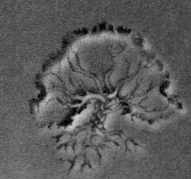

Future Generations

Highlights

My Prayers

2 CORINTHIANS 1:3-4

" 'JESUS CHRIST, THE FATHER OF

COMPASSION AND THE GOD OF ALL

COMFORT, 4WHO COMFORTS US IN ALL OUR

TROUBLES".

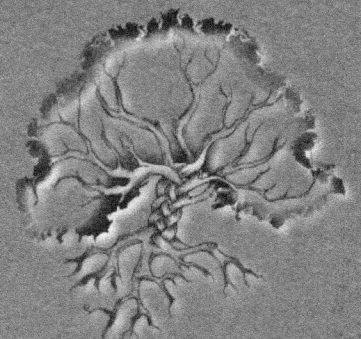

Thank You Lord

Week of: _____

 # Teach Me

_____
_____
_____
_____
_____
_____
_____
_____
_____

 # Guide Me

_____
_____
_____
_____
_____
_____
_____
_____
_____

 # Reflect

Scripture says faith is a gift. How are you sure that you

have accepted that gift?

Future Generations

Highlights

My Prayers

EPHESIANS 4:32

"BE KIND AND COMPASSIONATE TO ONE ANOTHER, FORGIVING EACH OTHER, JUST AS IN CHRIST GOD FORGAVE YOU".

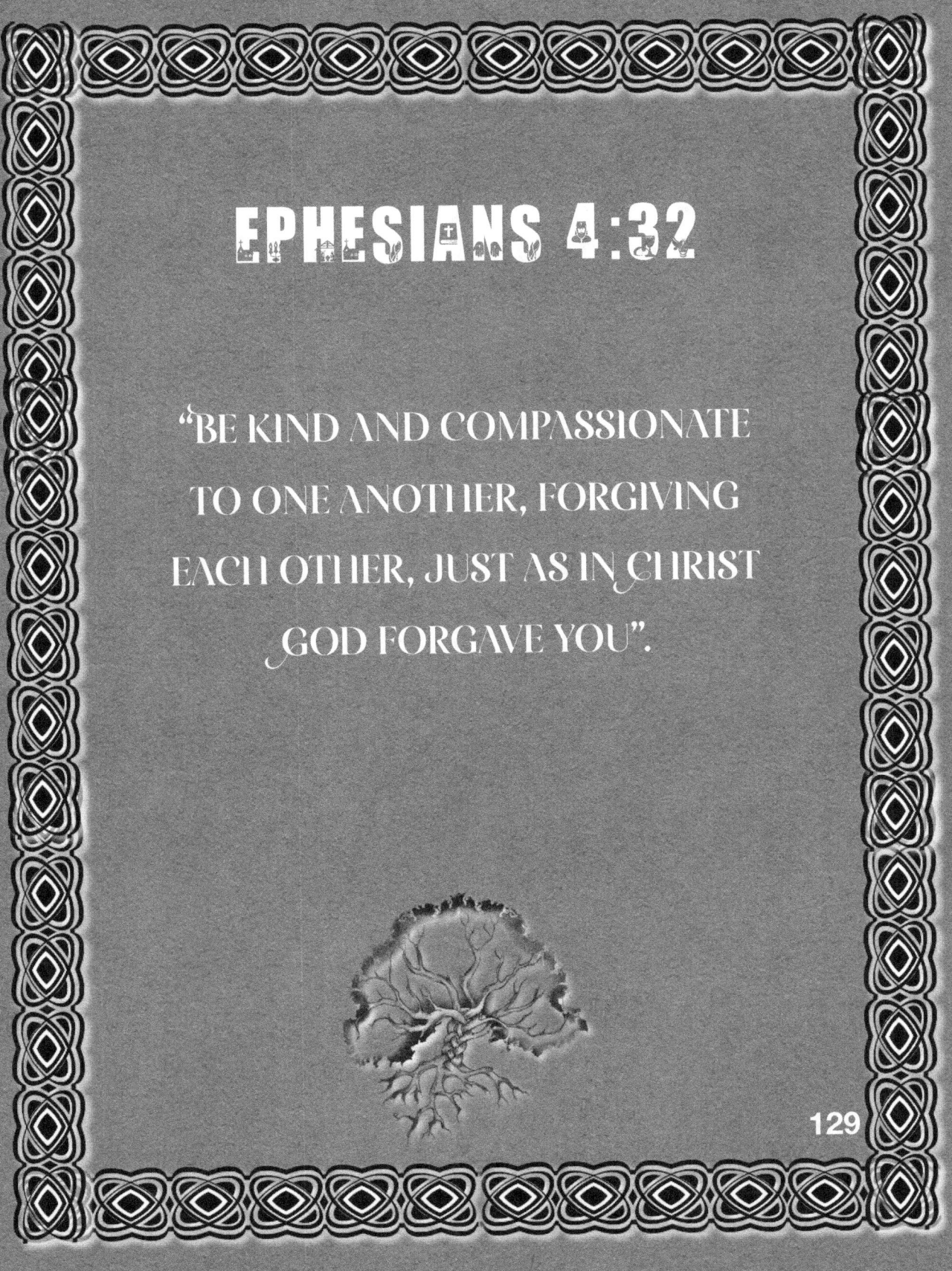

Thank You Lord

Week of: _____

 Teach Me

_____
_____
_____
_____
_____
_____
_____
_____

 Guide Me

_____
_____
_____
_____
_____
_____
_____
_____
_____

 # Reflect

What is one thing in your life that you are trying to keep

separate from God? Why do you think you are doing

that?

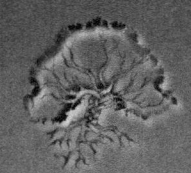
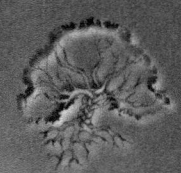

Future Generations

Highlights

My Prayers

ISAIAH 49:15

"CAN A WOMAN FORGET HER NURSING CHILD AND HAVE NO COMPASSION ON THE SON OF HER WOMB? EVEN THESE MAY FORGET, BUT I WILL NOT FORGET YOU".

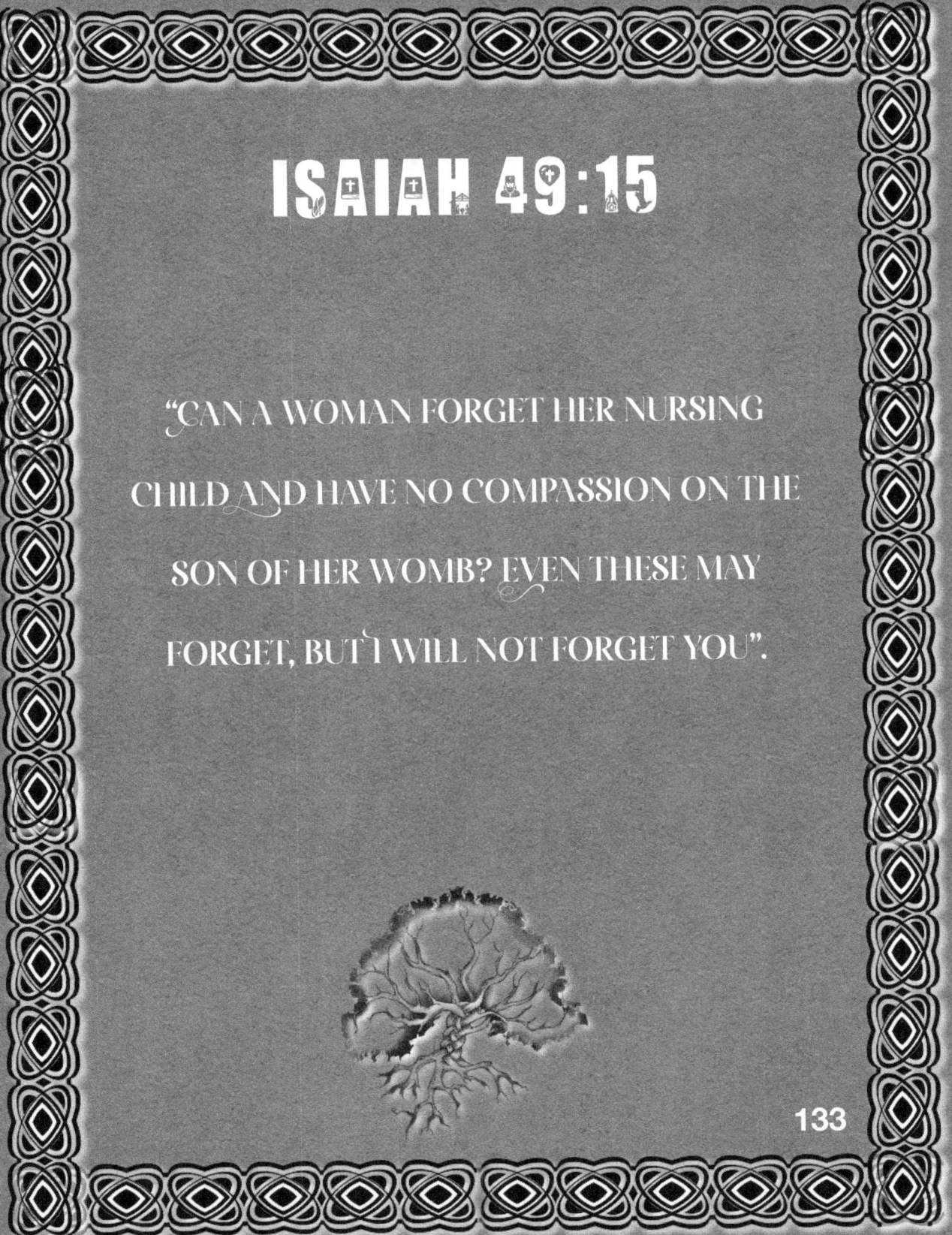

Thank You Lord

Week of: _____

 **Teach Me**

_____
_____
_____
_____
_____
_____
_____
_____

 Guide Me

_____
_____
_____
_____
_____
_____
_____

 # *Reflect*

What are 10 things that God has blessed you with? Try not to

think of the obvious things like good health and money for food.

Try to find the small pleasures that are often missed.

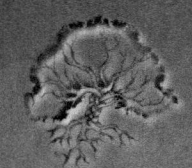
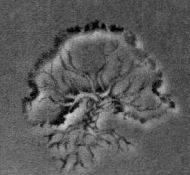

Future Generations

Highlights

My Prayers

1 CORINTHIANS 15:58

"THEREFORE, MY DEAR BROTHERS AND SISTERS, STAND FIRM. LET NOTHING MOVE YOU. ALWAYS GIVE YOURSELVES FULLY TO THE WORK OF THE LORD, BECAUSE YOU KNOW THAT YOUR LABOR IN THE LORD IS NOT IN VAIN".

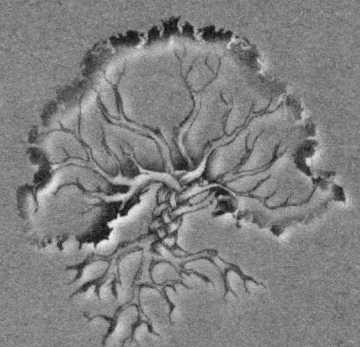

Thank You Lord

Week of: _____

 Teach Me

_____
_____
_____
_____
_____
_____
_____
_____

 Guide Me

_____
_____
_____
_____
_____
_____
_____
_____

 # *Reflect*

Was there a time recently when you wish you had gone to God first but didn't? What could you do differently next time so that you go to him first?

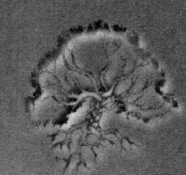

Future Generations

Highlights

My Prayers

CORINTHIANS 12:9

"TO ANOTHER FAITH BY THE SAME SPIRIT, TO ANOTHER GIFTS OF HEALING BY THAT ONE SPIRIT".

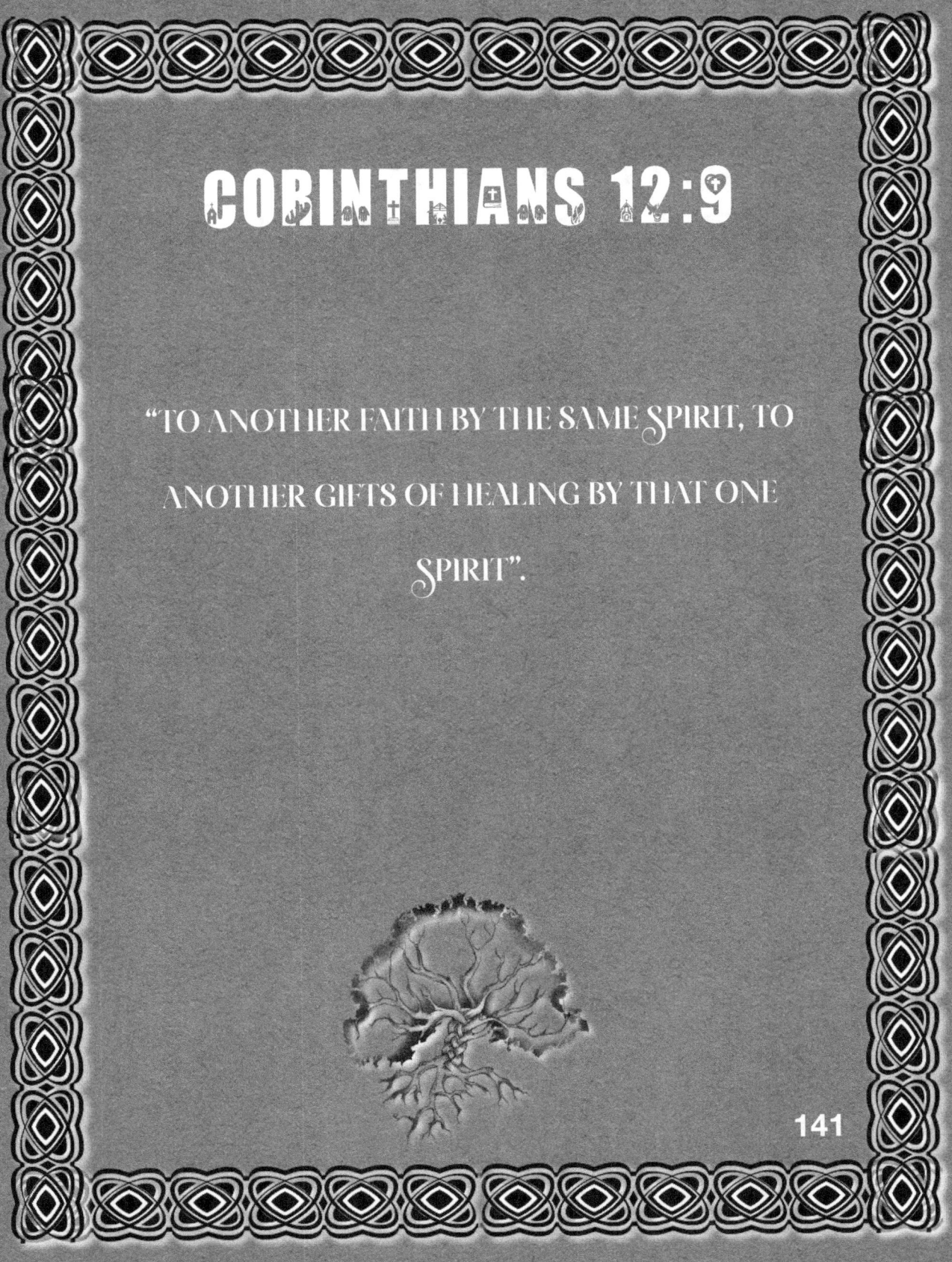

Thank You Lord

Week of: _____

 Teach Me

_____
_____
_____
_____
_____
_____
_____
_____
_____

Guide Me

_____
_____
_____
_____
_____
_____
_____
_____
_____

 # Reflect

Think of something bad that happened to you recently.

Consider five ways that God might use that bad thing for

something good.

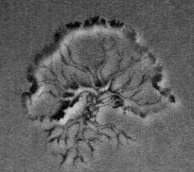

Future Generations

Highlights

My Prayers

ROMANS 8:38

"FOR I AM CONVINCED THAT NEITHER DEATH

NOR LIFE, NEITHER ANGELS NOR DEMONS,

NEITHER THE PRESENT NOR THE FUTURE, NOR

ANY POWERS, NEITHER HEIGHT NOR DEPTH,

NOR ANYTHING ELSE IN ALL CREATION, WILL BE

ABLE TO SEPARATE US FROM THE LOVE OF GOD

""THAT IS IN CHRIST JESUS OUR LORD".

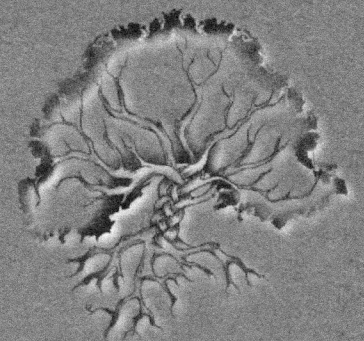

Thank You Lord

Week of: _____

 Teach Me

_____
_____
_____
_____
_____
_____
_____
_____
_____
_____

 Guide Me

_____
_____
_____
_____
_____
_____
_____
_____
_____
_____
_____

 # Reflect

If you could come up with *one word* that would sum up this season of your life, what would it be? Why did you choose that word?

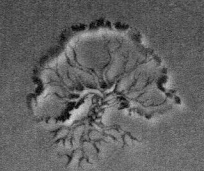
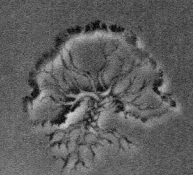

Future Generations

Highlights

My Prayers

LUKE 16:13

"NO ONE CAN SERVE TWO MASTERS. EITHER YOU WILL HATE THE ONE AND LOVE THE OTHER, OR YOU WILL BE DEVOTED TO THE ONE AND DESPISE THE OTHER. YOU CANNOT SERVE BOTH GOD AND MONEY.".

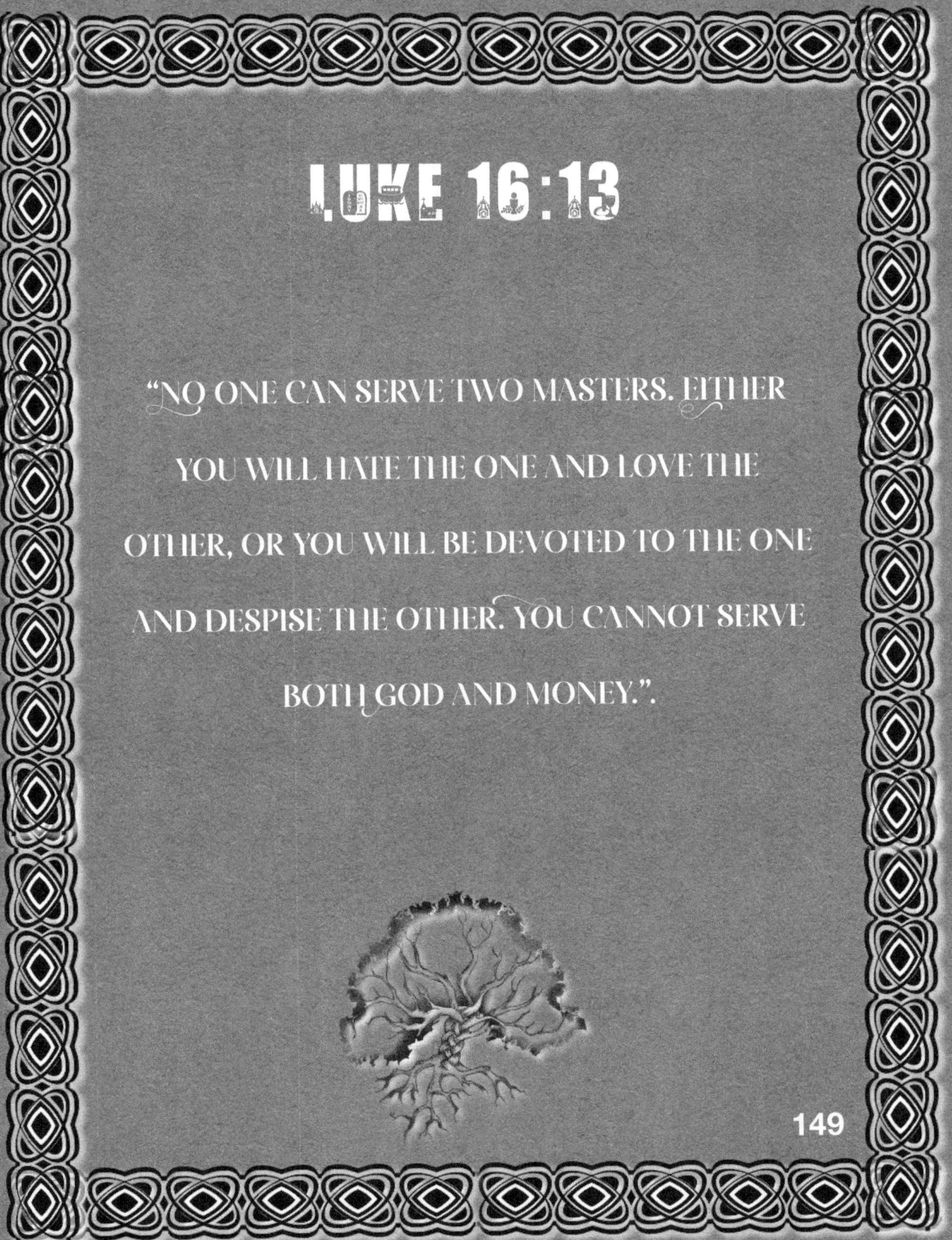

Thank You Lord

 Teach Me

Guide Me

 # Reflect

Think of a song, a movie, or an event that has encouraged you recently. Why do you think it spoke to you? What do you think God is trying to tell you?

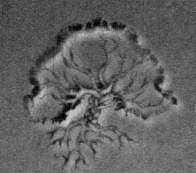 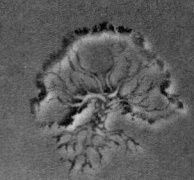

Future Generations

Highlights

My Prayers

152

JEREMIAH 17:7-8

"BLESSED IS THE ONE WHO TRUSTS IN THE LORD,

WHOSE CONFIDENCE IS IN HIM.

THEY WILL BE LIKE A TREE PLANTED BY THE

WATER THAT SENDS OUT ITS ROOTS BY THE

STREAM.IT DOES NOT FEAR WHEN HEAT COMES;

ITS LEAVES ARE ALWAYS GREEN.

IT HAS NO WORRIES IN A YEAR OF DROUGHT

AND NEVER FAILS TO BEAR FRUIT".

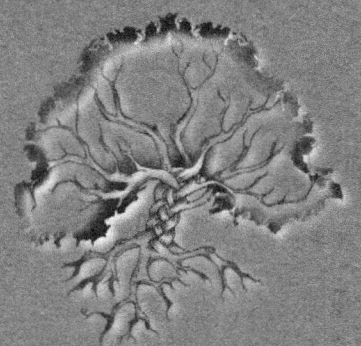

Thank You Lord

Week of: _____

🌳 **Teach Me** 🌳

_____
_____
_____
_____
_____
_____
_____
_____

🌳 **Guide Me** 🌳

_____
_____
_____
_____
_____
_____
_____
_____

 # Reflect

What are some lies you have been believing lately about your own life? Find a Bible verse that corrects these lies and reminds you of the truth.

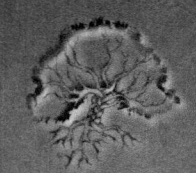

Future Generations

Highlights

My Prayers

GALATIANS 5:22-23

"BUT THE FRUIT OF THE SPIRIT IS LOVE, JOY, PEACE, FORBEARANCE, KINDNESS, GOODNESS, FAITHFULNESS, GENTLENESS AND SELF-CONTROL. AGAINST SUCH THINGS THERE IS NO LAW".

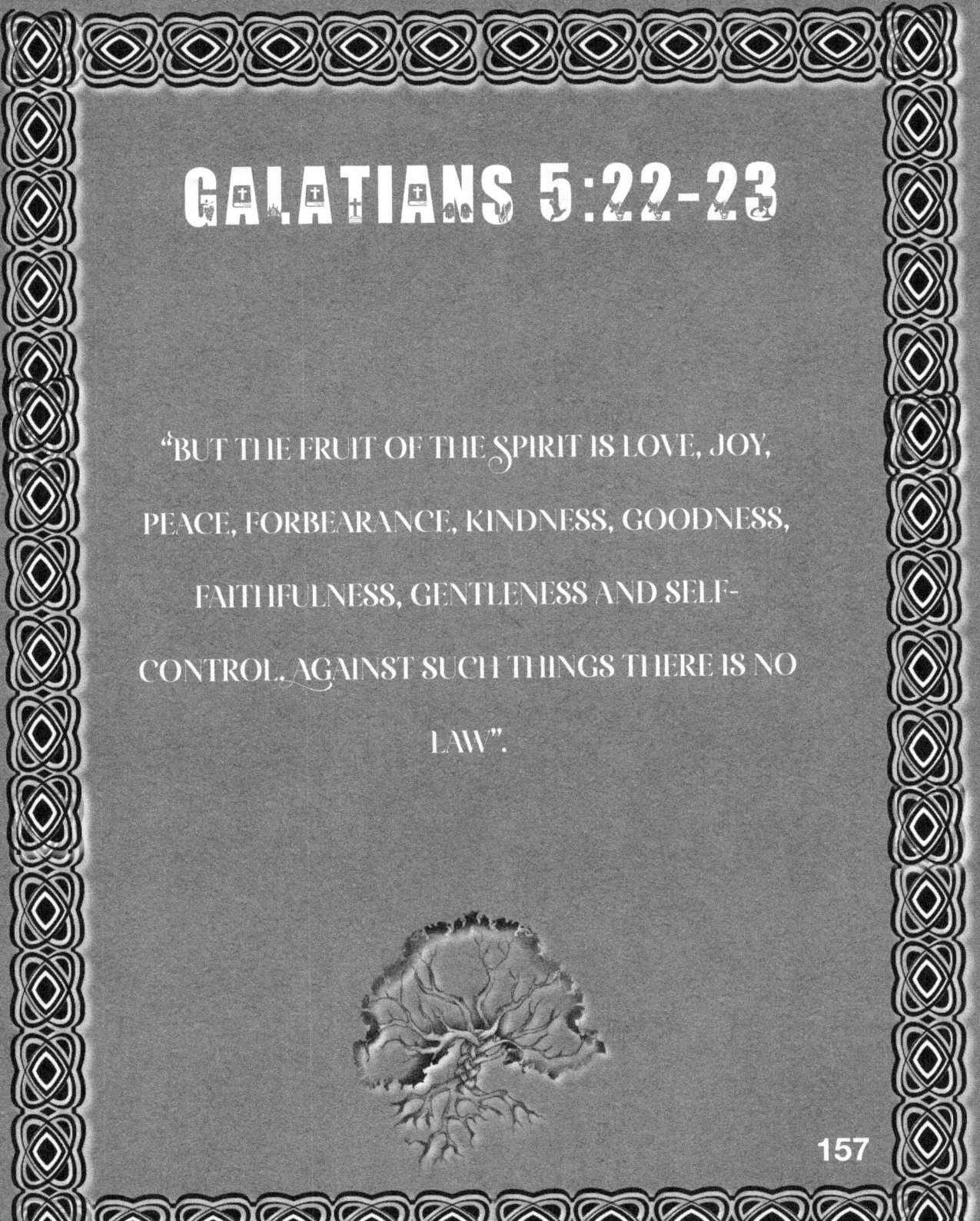

Thank You Lord

Week of: _____

 # Teach Me

_____
_____
_____
_____
_____
_____
_____
_____
_____

 # Guide Me

_____
_____
_____
_____
_____
_____
_____
_____
_____

 # Reflect

Read some of your old reflections. How has God shown up for you in the past that can make you feel more confident that he will show up for you now?

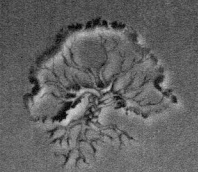 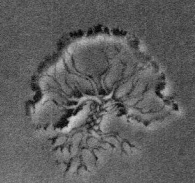

Future Generations

Highlights

My Prayers

EPHESIANS 4:26-27

"IN YOUR ANGER DO NOT SIN": DO NOT LET THE SUN GO DOWN WHILE YOU ARE STILL ANGRY, AND DO NOT GIVE THE DEVIL A FOOTHOLD".

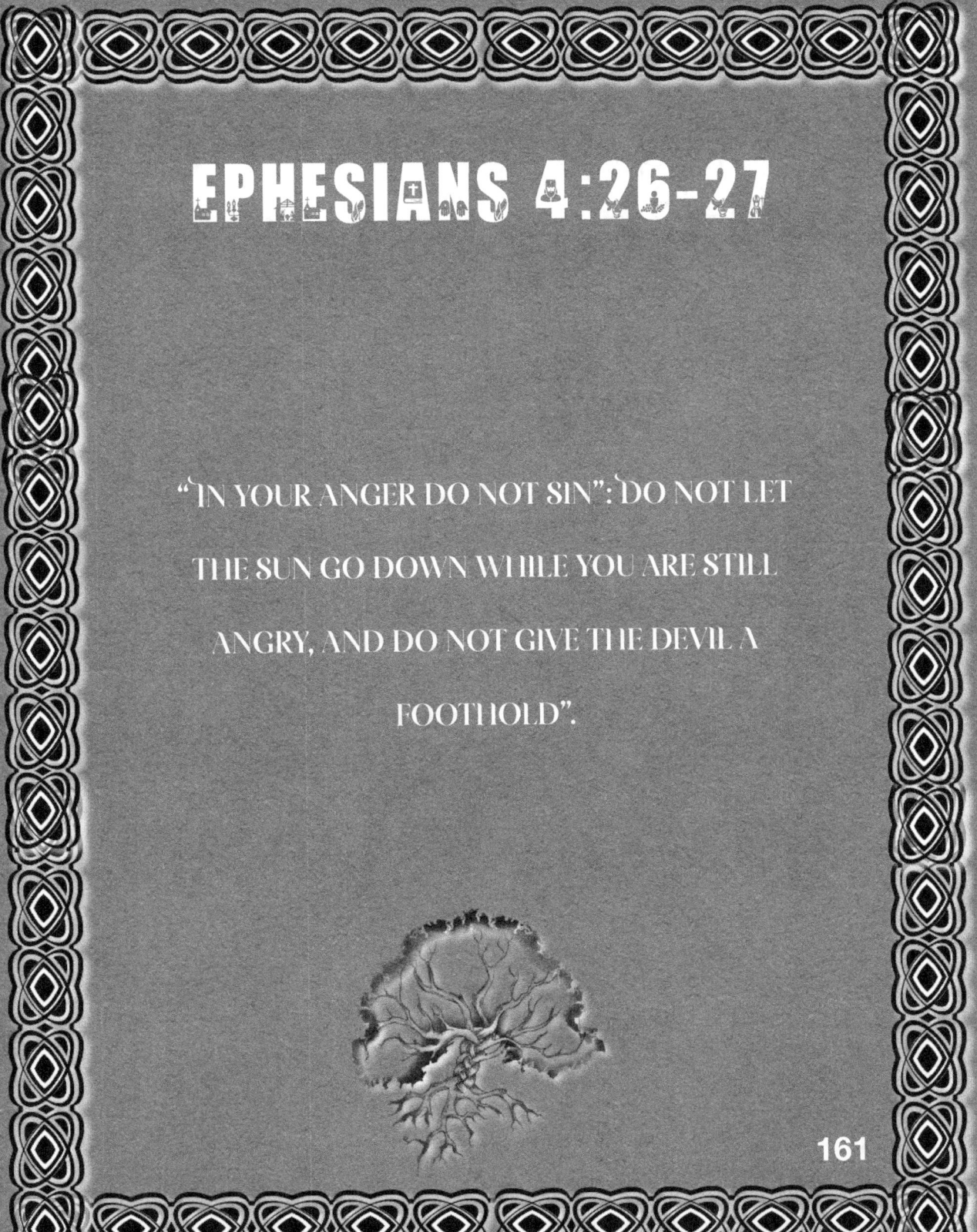

Thank You Lord

Week of: _____

 Teach Me

_____
_____
_____
_____
_____
_____
_____
_____
_____
_____
_____
_____

Guide Me

_____
_____
_____
_____
_____
_____
_____
_____
_____
_____
_____
_____

Reflect

Think of a time in your life when you thought God had left you alone. Looking back, do you see what he was doing to help you in this season?

_____
_____
_____
_____
_____
_____
_____
_____
_____
_____
_____
_____
_____
_____
_____
_____
_____
_____
_____
_____
_____
_____
_____

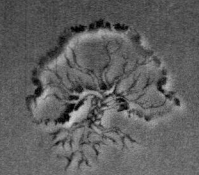

Future Generations

Highlights

My Prayers

COLOSSIANS 3:15

"AND LET THE PEACE OF CHRIST RULE IN YOUR HEARTS, TO WHICH INDEED YOU WERE CALLED IN ONE BODY. AND BE THANKFUL".

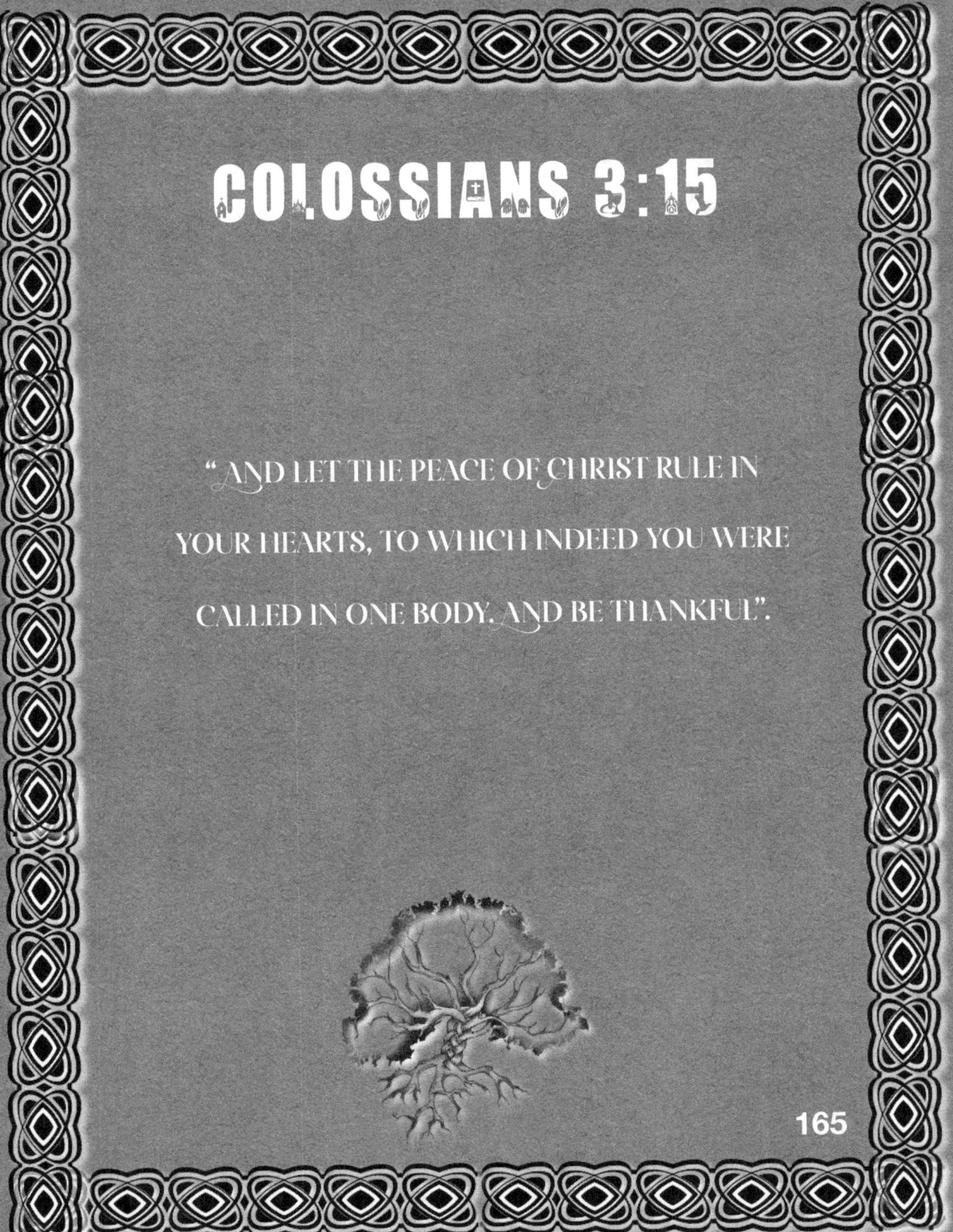

Thank You Lord

 Teach Me

 Guide Me

 # Reflect

What is something happening right now that you can't

accomplish without God's help?

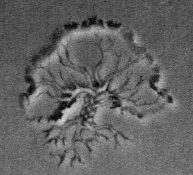
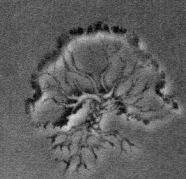

Future Generations

Highlights

My Prayers

JAMES 4:2

"YOU DESIRE BUT DO NOT HAVE, SO YOU KILL. YOU COVET BUT YOU CANNOT GET WHAT YOU WANT, SO YOU QUARREL AND FIGHT. YOU DO NOT HAVE BECAUSE YOU DO NOT ASK GOD".

Thank You Lord

Week of: _____

 Teach Me

_____
_____
_____
_____
_____
_____
_____
_____
_____
_____

 Guide Me

_____
_____
_____
_____
_____
_____
_____
_____
_____

 # Reflect

Think of a time in your life when you thought God had left you alone. Looking back, do you see what he was doing to help you in this season?

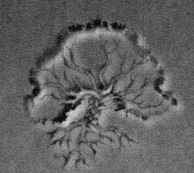
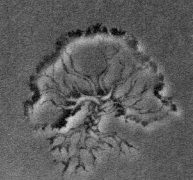

Future Generations

Highlights

My Prayers

CORINTHIANS 10:13

"NO TEMPTATION HAS OVERTAKEN YOU

EXCEPT WHAT IS COMMON TO MANKIND.

AND GOD IS FAITHFUL; HE WILL NOT LET YOU

BE TEMPTED BEYOND WHAT YOU CAN BEAR.

BUT WHEN YOU ARE TEMPTED, HE WILL ALSO

PROVIDE A WAY OUT SO THAT YOU CAN

ENDURE IT".

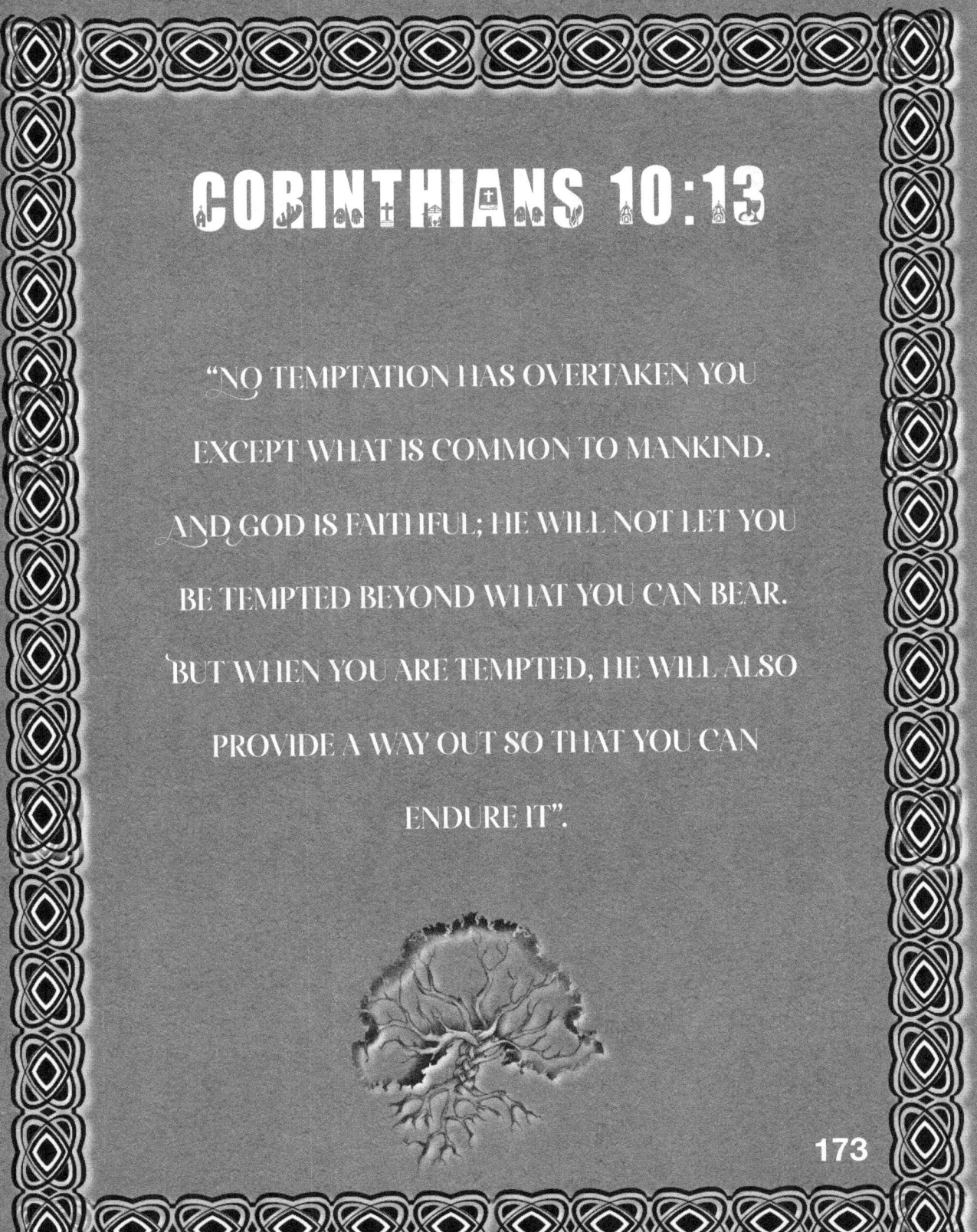

Thank You Lord

Week of: _____

 # Teach Me

_____
_____
_____
_____
_____
_____
_____
_____
_____
_____

Guide Me

_____
_____
_____
_____
_____
_____
_____
_____
_____
_____

 # Reflect

Do you think faith and logic have anything to do with each other? What Bible verses can you use to support your thoughts?

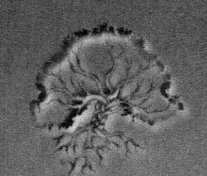

Future Generations

Highlights

My Prayers

1 TIMOTHY 6:7-8

"FOR WE BROUGHT NOTHING INTO THE

WORLD, AND WE CAN TAKE NOTHING OUT OF

IT. BUT IF WE HAVE FOOD AND CLOTHING, WE

WILL BE CONTENT WITH THAT"

".

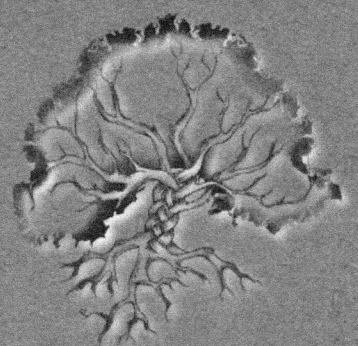

Thank You Lord

Week of: _____

 # Teach Me

_____
_____
_____
_____
_____
_____
_____
_____
_____
_____
_____
_____

 # Guide Me

_____
_____
_____
_____
_____
_____
_____
_____
_____
_____
_____

 # Reflect

Is there a Bible verse or a phrase that God has been bringing to your mind a lot lately? What do you think you should do with that information?

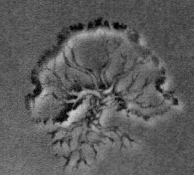

Future Generations

Highlights

My Prayers

MATTHEW 6:19-20

"DO NOT STORE UP FOR YOURSELVES TREASURES ON EARTH, WHERE MOTHS AND VERMIN DESTROY, AND WHERE THIEVES BREAK IN AND STEAL. BUT STORE UP FOR YOURSELVES TREASURES IN HEAVEN, WHERE MOTHS AND VERMIN DO NOT DESTROY, AND WHERE THIEVES DO NOT BREAK IN AND STEAL"

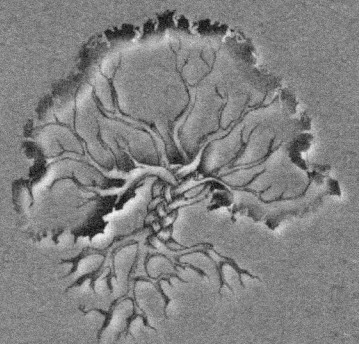

Thank You Lord

Week of: _____

 Teach Me

_____
_____
_____
_____
_____
_____
_____
_____
_____
_____
_____

 Guide Me

_____
_____
_____
_____
_____
_____
_____
_____
_____

 # Reflect

What has happened this past month that you wouldn't have been able to do without God's help. How do you know you couldn't have done it without him?

_____
_____
_____
_____
_____
_____
_____
_____
_____
_____
_____
_____
_____
_____
_____
_____
_____
_____
_____
_____
_____
_____

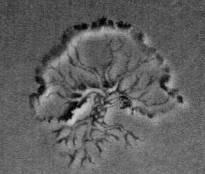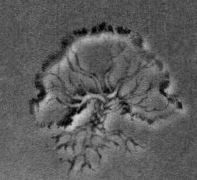

Future Generations

Highlights

My Prayers

ROMANS 1:20

"FOR SINCE THE CREATION OF THE WORLD GOD'S INVISIBLE QUALITIES—HIS ETERNAL POWER AND DIVINE NATURE—HAVE BEEN CLEARLY SEEN, BEING UNDERSTOOD FROM WHAT HAS BEEN MADE, SO THAT PEOPLE ARE WITHOUT EXCUSE".

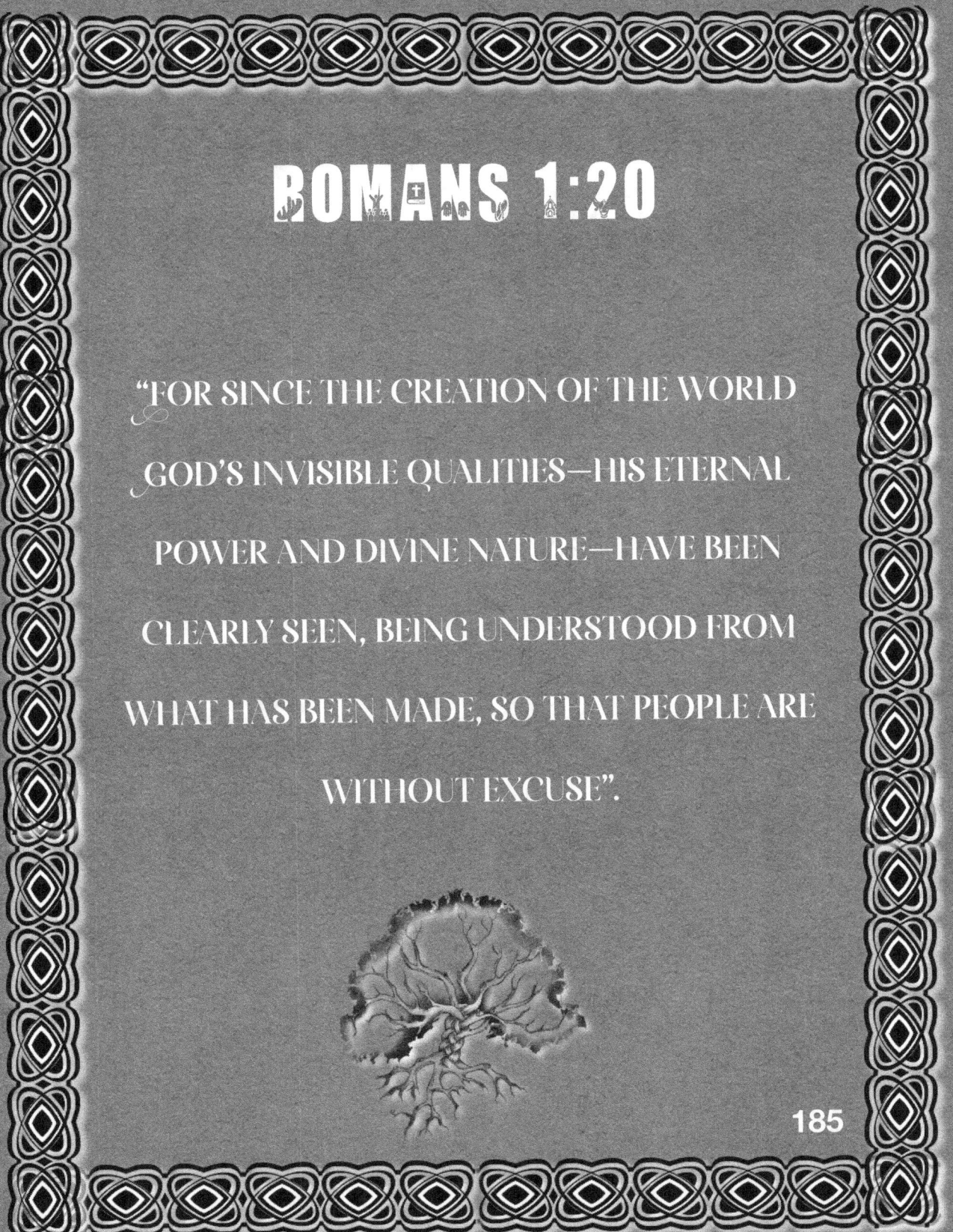

Thank You Lord

 Teach Me

 Guide Me

 # Reflect

Do you feel like you are expecting too much from God? Or do you

feel like you are expecting too little from him? Why do you feel

that way?

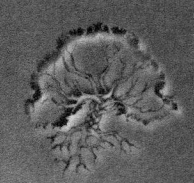

Future Generations

Highlights

My Prayers

GENESIS 1:26

"THEN GOD SAID, "LET US MAKE MANKIND IN OUR IMAGE, IN OUR LIKENESS, SO THAT THEY MAY RULE OVER THE FISH IN THE SEA AND THE BIRDS IN THE SKY, OVER THE LIVESTOCK AND ALL THE WILD ANIMALS, AND OVER ALL THE CREATURES THAT MOVE ALONG THE GROUND".

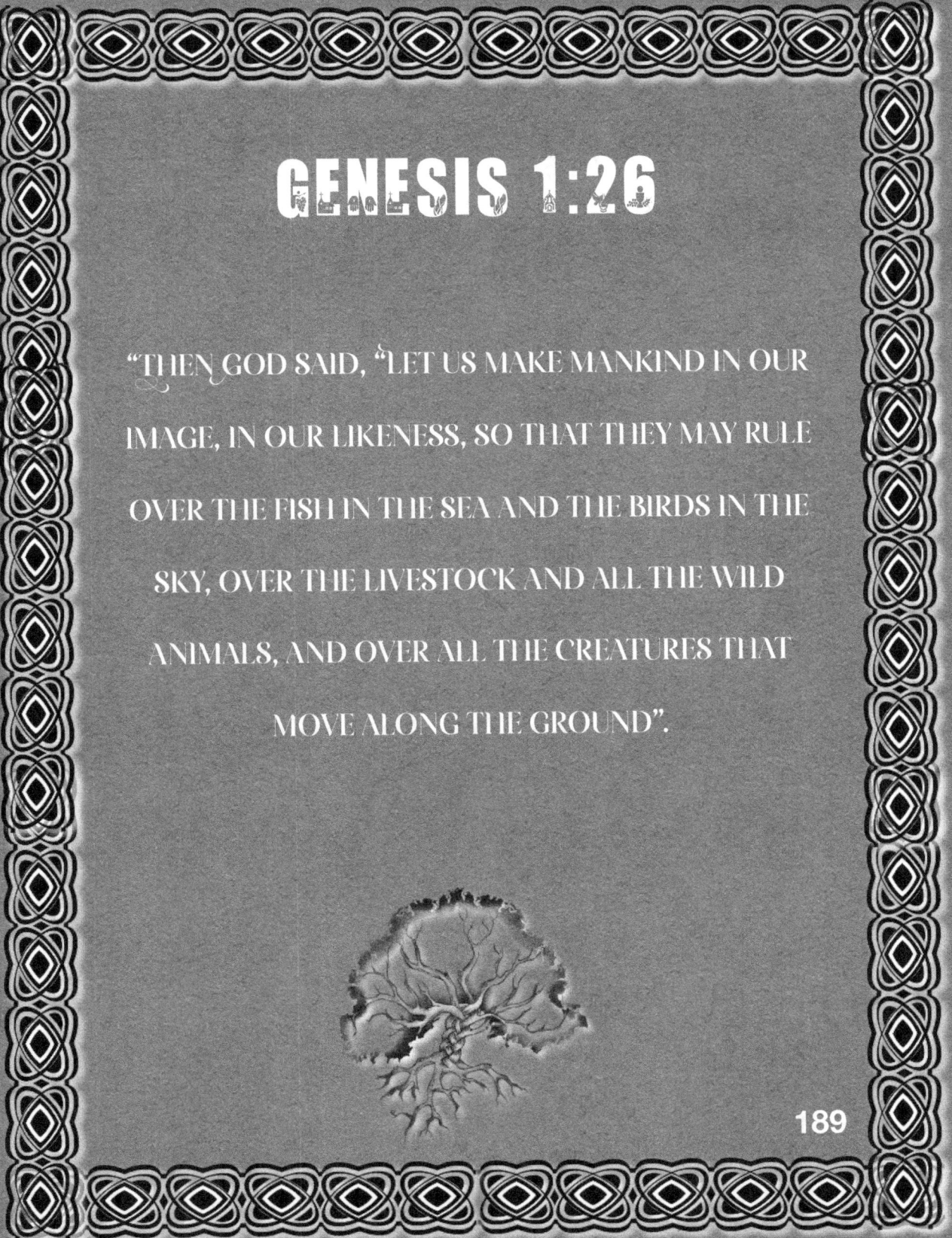

Thank You Lord

Week of: _____

 Teach Me

_____
_____
_____
_____
_____
_____
_____
_____

 Guide Me

_____
_____
_____
_____
_____
_____
_____
_____

 # Reflect

When you talk to God, do you feel like you are holding back or are you acting like yourself when you talk to him?

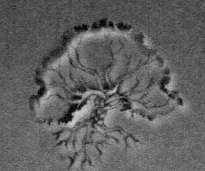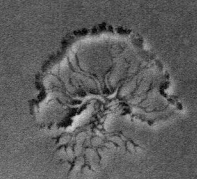

Future Generations

Highlights

My Prayers

ECCLESIASTES 11:5

"AS YOU DO NOT KNOW THE PATH OF THE

WIND,

OR HOW THE BODY IS FORMED IN A

MOTHER'S WOMB, SO YOU CANNOT

UNDERSTAND THE WORK OF GOD, THE

MAKER OF ALL THINGS".

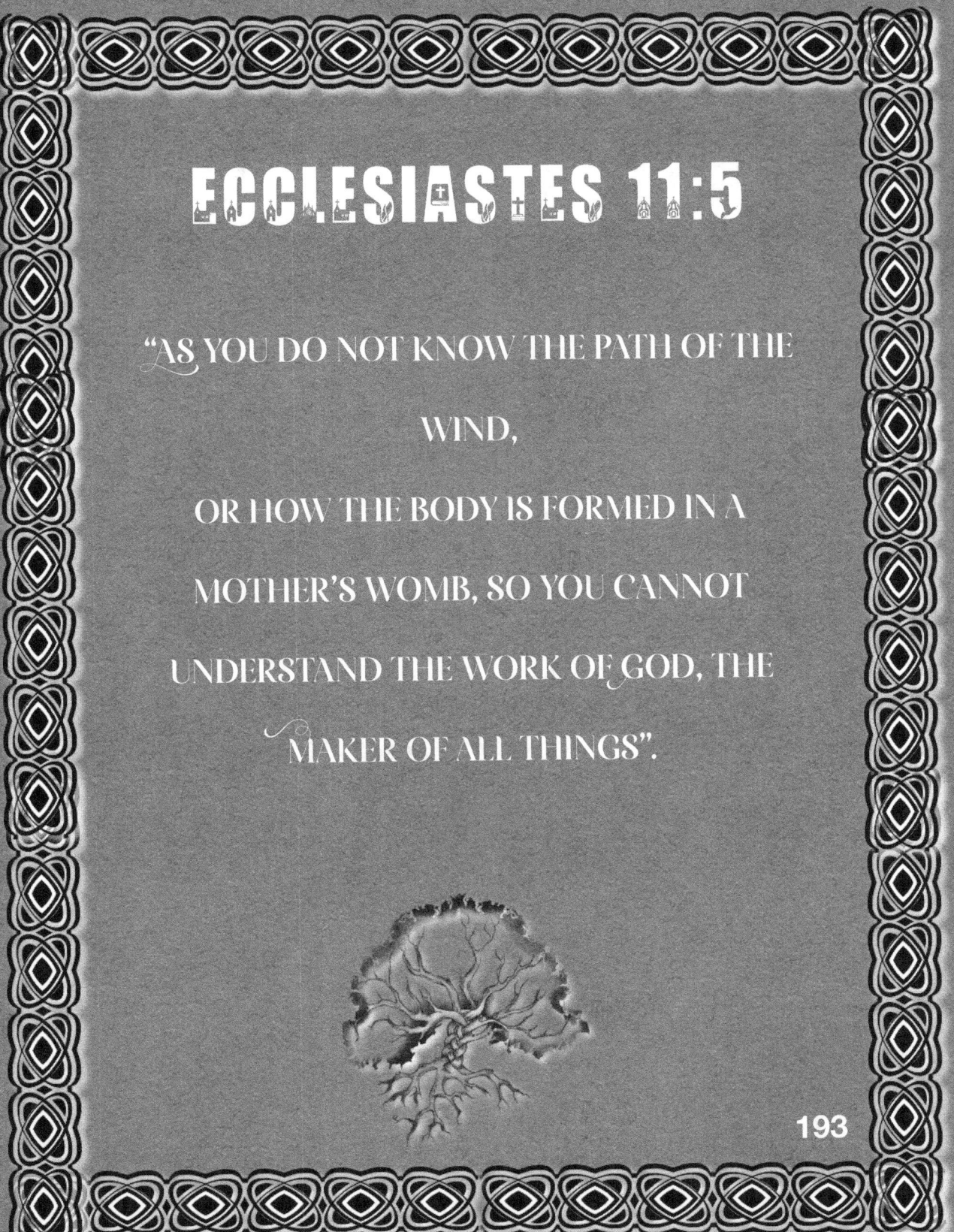

Thank You Lord

Week of:

Teach Me

Guide Me

 # Reflect

What specific prayers, big or small, has God

answered recently?

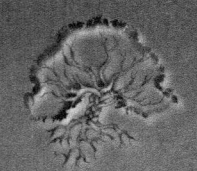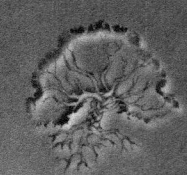

Future Generations

Highlights

My Prayers

2 CORINTHIANS 4:18

"SO WE FIX OUR EYES NOT ON WHAT IS SEEN, BUT ON WHAT IS UNSEEN, SINCE WHAT IS SEEN IS TEMPORARY, BUT WHAT IS UNSEEN IS ETERNAL".

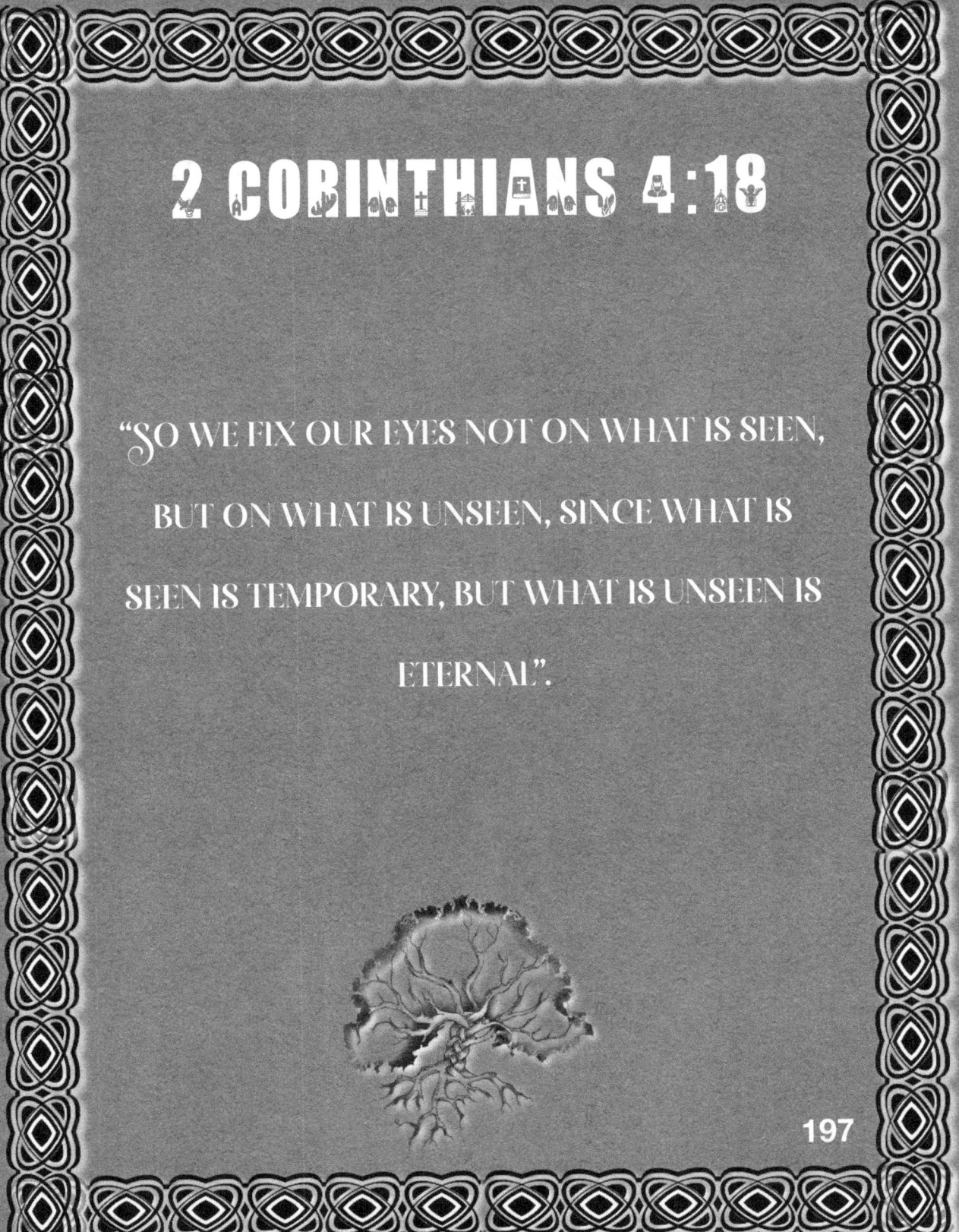

Thank You Lord

Week of: _____

♥ Teach Me ♥

_____
_____
_____
_____
_____
_____
_____
_____

♥ Guide Me ♥

_____
_____
_____
_____
_____
_____
_____
_____

 # Reflect

Write about a time when God sent you a direct

message you couldn't miss.

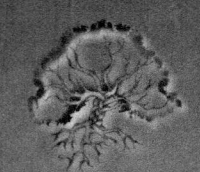
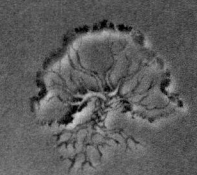

Future Generations

Highlights

My Prayers

COLOSSIANS 3:16

"LET THE MESSAGE OF CHRIST DWELL AMONG YOU RICHLY AS YOU TEACH AND ADMONISH ONE ANOTHER WITH ALL WISDOM THROUGH PSALMS, HYMNS, AND SONGS FROM THE SPIRIT, SINGING TO GOD WITH GRATITUDE IN YOUR HEARTS".

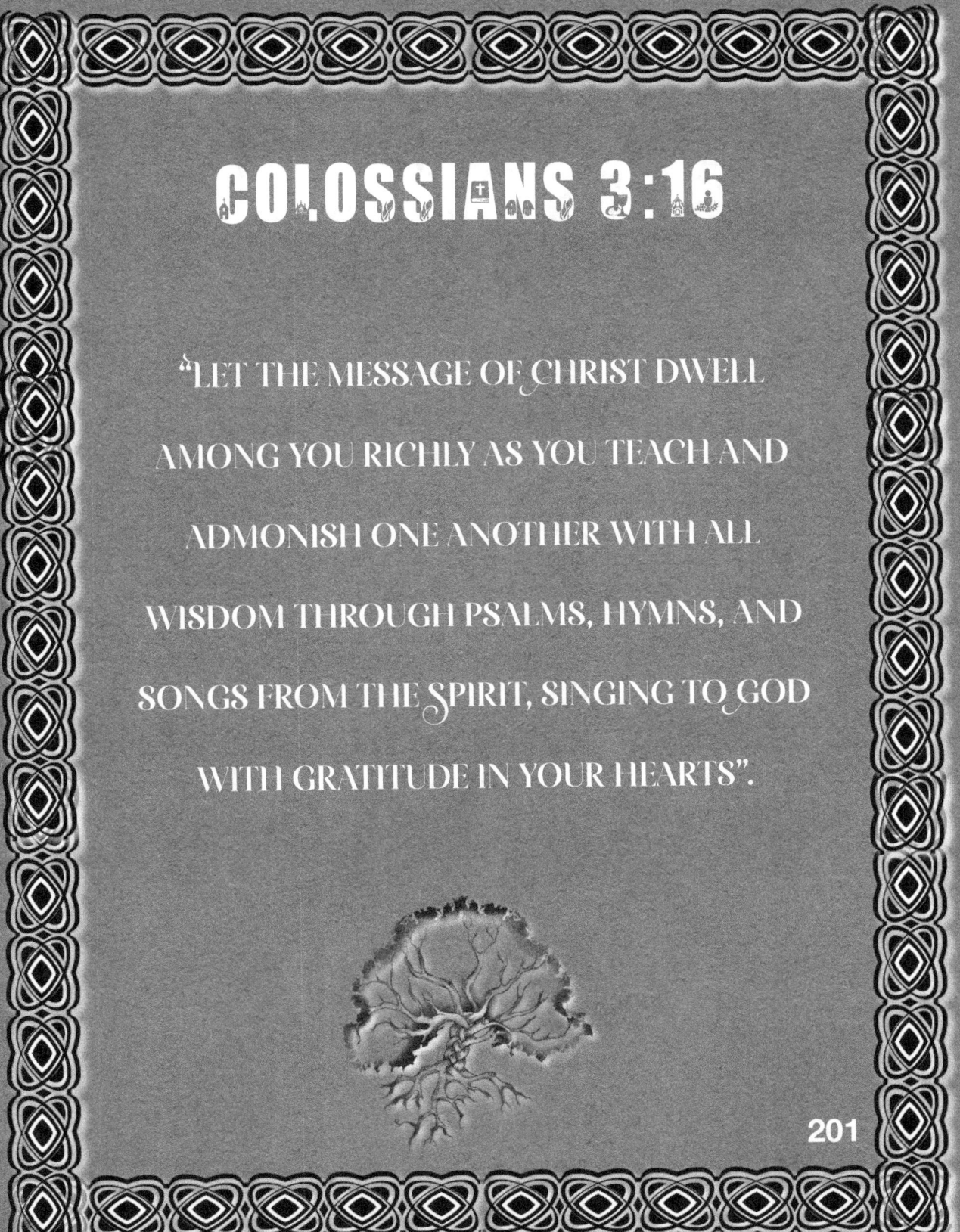

Thank You Lord

Week of: _____

 # Teach Me

_____
_____
_____
_____
_____
_____
_____
_____
_____

 # Guide Me

_____
_____
_____
_____
_____
_____
_____
_____

 # Reflect

The Israelites in Ezekiel's day complained about God being unjust and life being unfair, just as people today do. People ask how God could send someone to hell-especially a person who is trying to do good. Each one of us has sinned, and as a result, we deserve punishment. It is only through God's grace and Jesus' sacrificial death that people can ask for forgiveness and be saved. How do you define justice? How do you define grace?

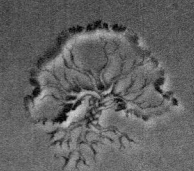
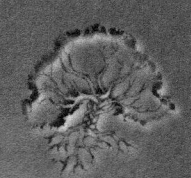

Future Generations

Highlights

My Prayers

1 JOHN 2:27

AS FOR YOU, THE ANOINTING YOU RECEIVED FROM HIM REMAINS IN YOU, AND YOU DO NOT NEED ANYONE TO TEACH YOU. BUT AS HIS ANOINTING TEACHES YOU ABOUT ALL THINGS AND AS THAT ANOINTING IS REAL, NOT COUNTERFEIT—JUST AS IT HAS TAUGHT YOU, REMAIN IN HIM.

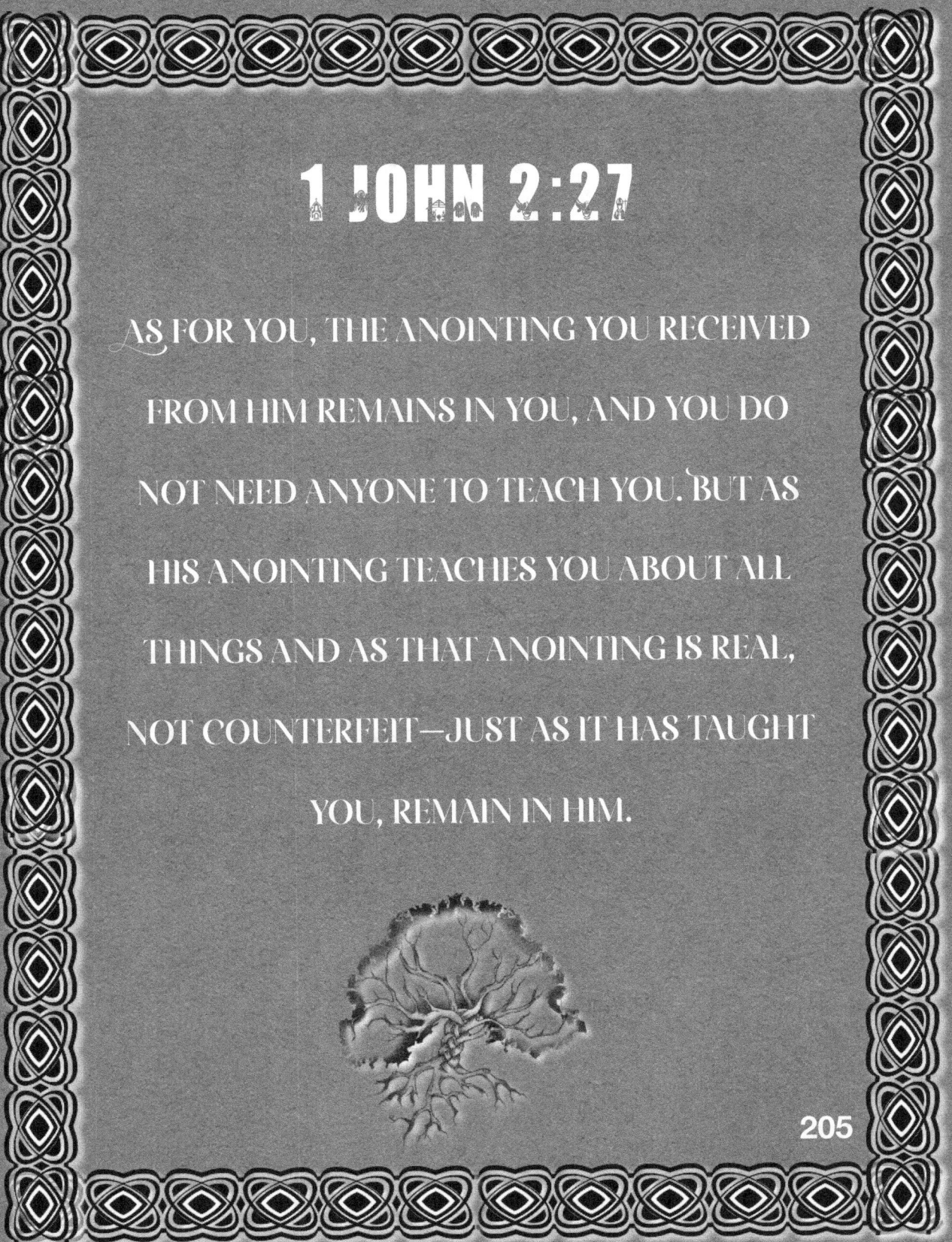

Thank You Lord

Week of: _____

 Teach Me

_____
_____
_____
_____
_____
_____
_____
_____
_____
_____

 Guide Me

_____
_____
_____
_____
_____
_____
_____
_____
_____
_____
_____

 # Reflect

How are the spaces in which you spend time with God? Is your work, home, and car set up to support your faith?

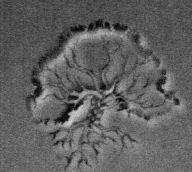
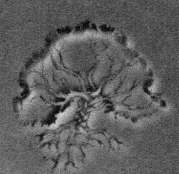

Future Generations

Highlights

My Prayers

MARK 10:27

"JESUS LOOKED AT THEM AND SAID, "WITH MAN THIS IS IMPOSSIBLE, BUT NOT WITH GOD; ALL THINGS ARE POSSIBLE WITH GOD".

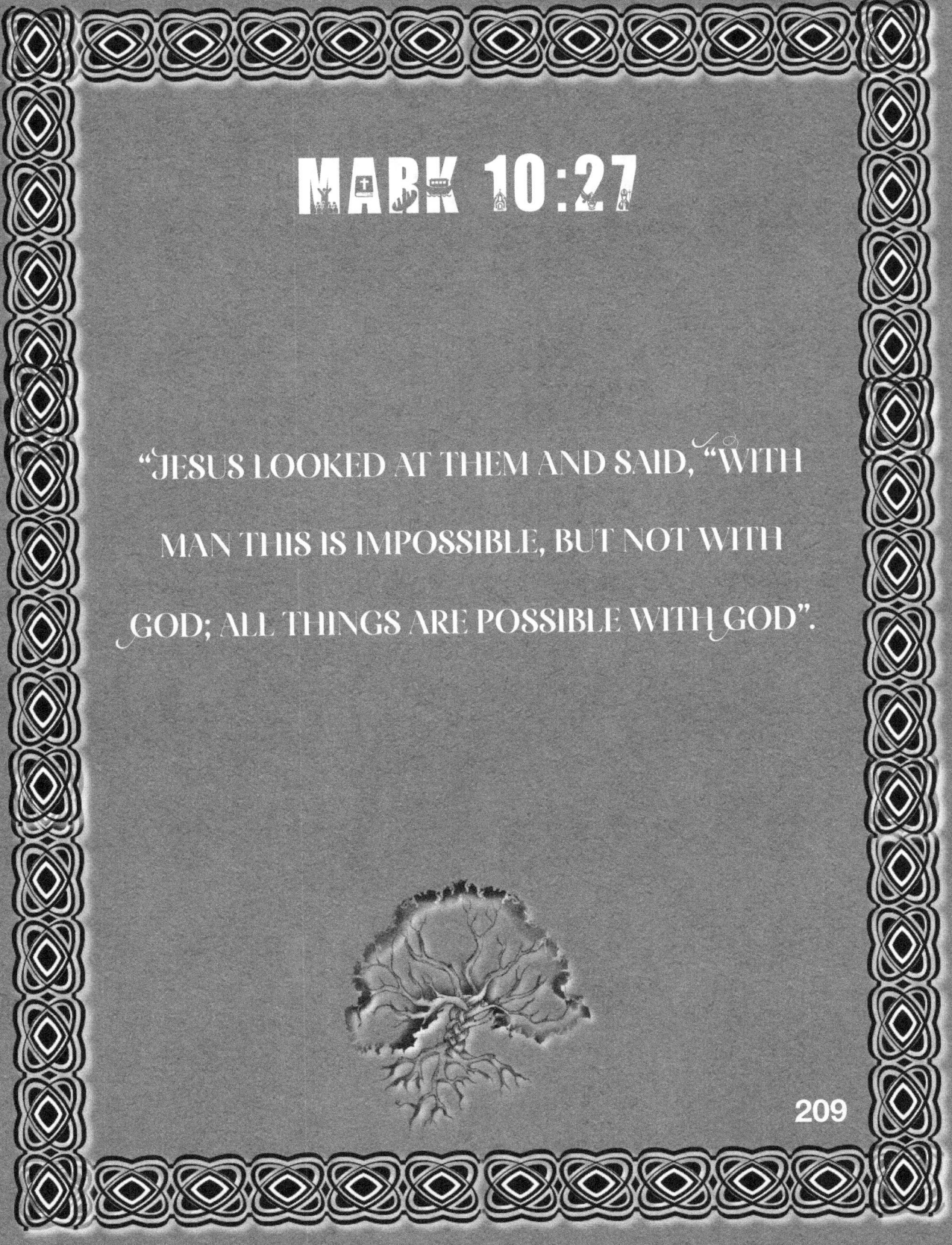

Thank You Lord

Week of: _____

 ## Teach Me

_____
_____
_____
_____
_____
_____
_____
_____
_____
_____

 ## Guide Me

_____
_____
_____
_____
_____
_____
_____
_____
_____
_____
_____

 # *Reflect*

When was the last time you
encouraged someone in their faith?
How did it go? How did it impact
you?

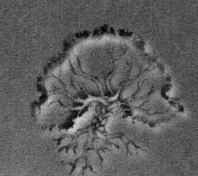

Future Generations

Highlights

My Prayers

MATTHEW 17:20

"He replied, "Because you have so little faith. Truly I tell you, if you have faith as small as a mustard seed, you can say to this mountain, 'Move from here to there,' and it will move. Nothing will be impossible for you".

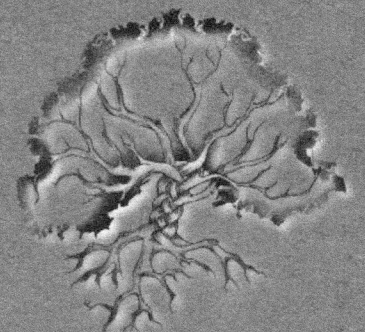

Thank You Lord

Week of:

 # Teach Me

 # Guide Me

Reflect

> ## Romans 8:28
>
> " We know that all things work together for good to those who love
>
> God, to those who are the called according to His purpose"
>
> **Life hardly ever takes a straight path. What does this passage say about all the detours your life might take?**

Future Generations

Highlights

My Prayers

JOHN 10:28

"I GIVE ETERNAL LIFE TO THEM, AND THEY WILL NEVER PERISH; AND NO ONE WILL SNATCH THEM OUT OF MY HAND. 29"MY FATHER, WHO HAS GIVEN THEM TO ME, IS GREATER THAN ALL; AND NO ONE IS ABLE TO SNATCH THEM OUT OF THE FATHER'S HAND. 30"I AND THE FATHER ARE ONE".

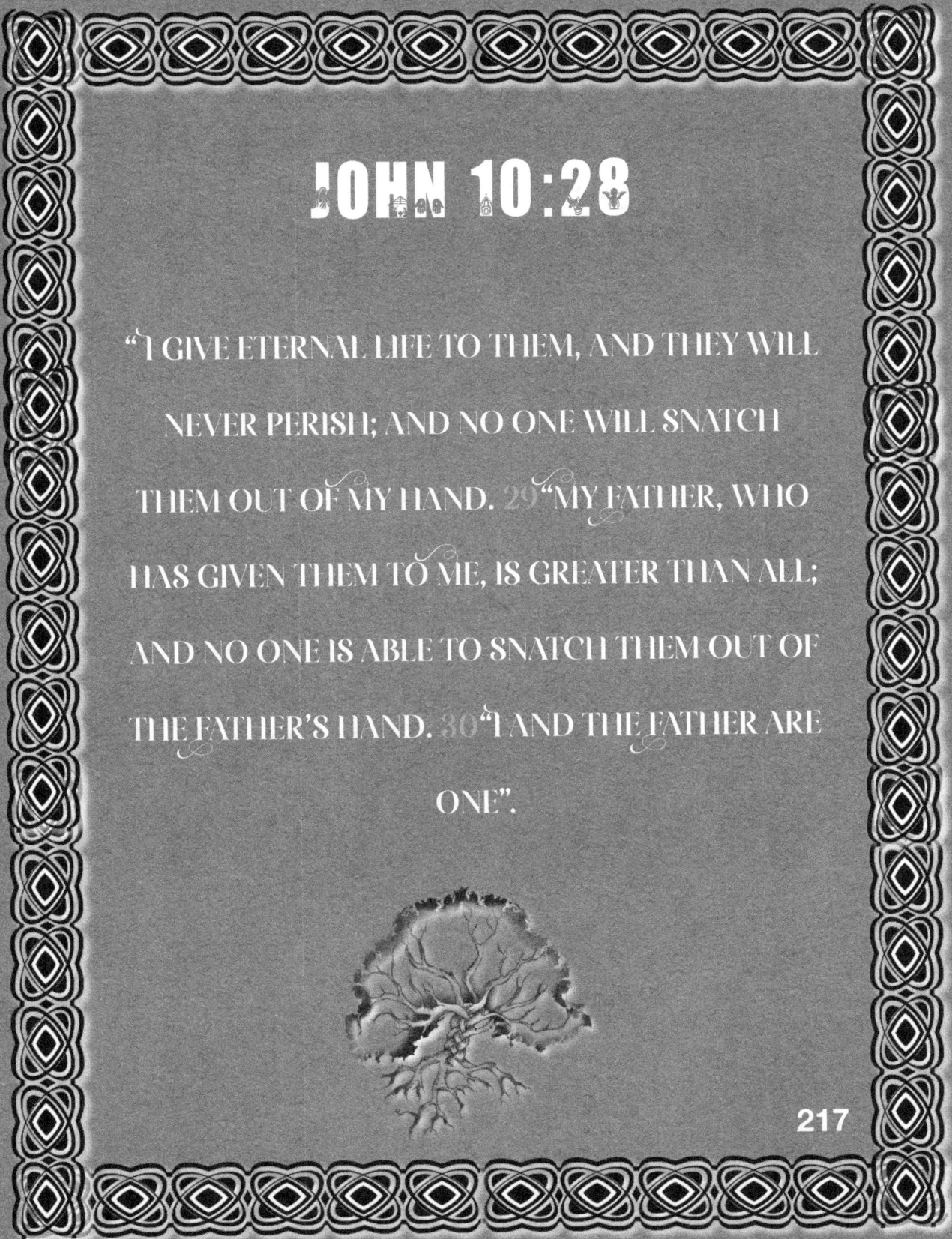

Thank You Lord

Week of: _____

 # Teach Me

 # Guide Me

 # Reflect

Stepping out in faith isn't always easy. What would you tell someone who is about to step out on faith?

_____
_____
_____
_____
_____
_____
_____
_____
_____
_____
_____
_____
_____
_____
_____
_____
_____
_____
_____
_____
_____

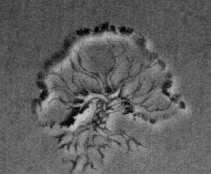
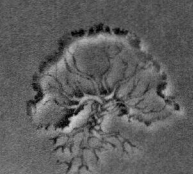

Future Generations

Highlights

My Prayers

1 TIMOTHY 6:12

" FIGHT THE GOOD FIGHT OF THE FAITH.
TAKE HOLD OF THE ETERNAL LIFE TO
WHICH YOU WERE CALLED WHEN YOU
MADE YOUR GOOD CONFESSION IN THE
PRESENCE OF MANY WITNESSES".

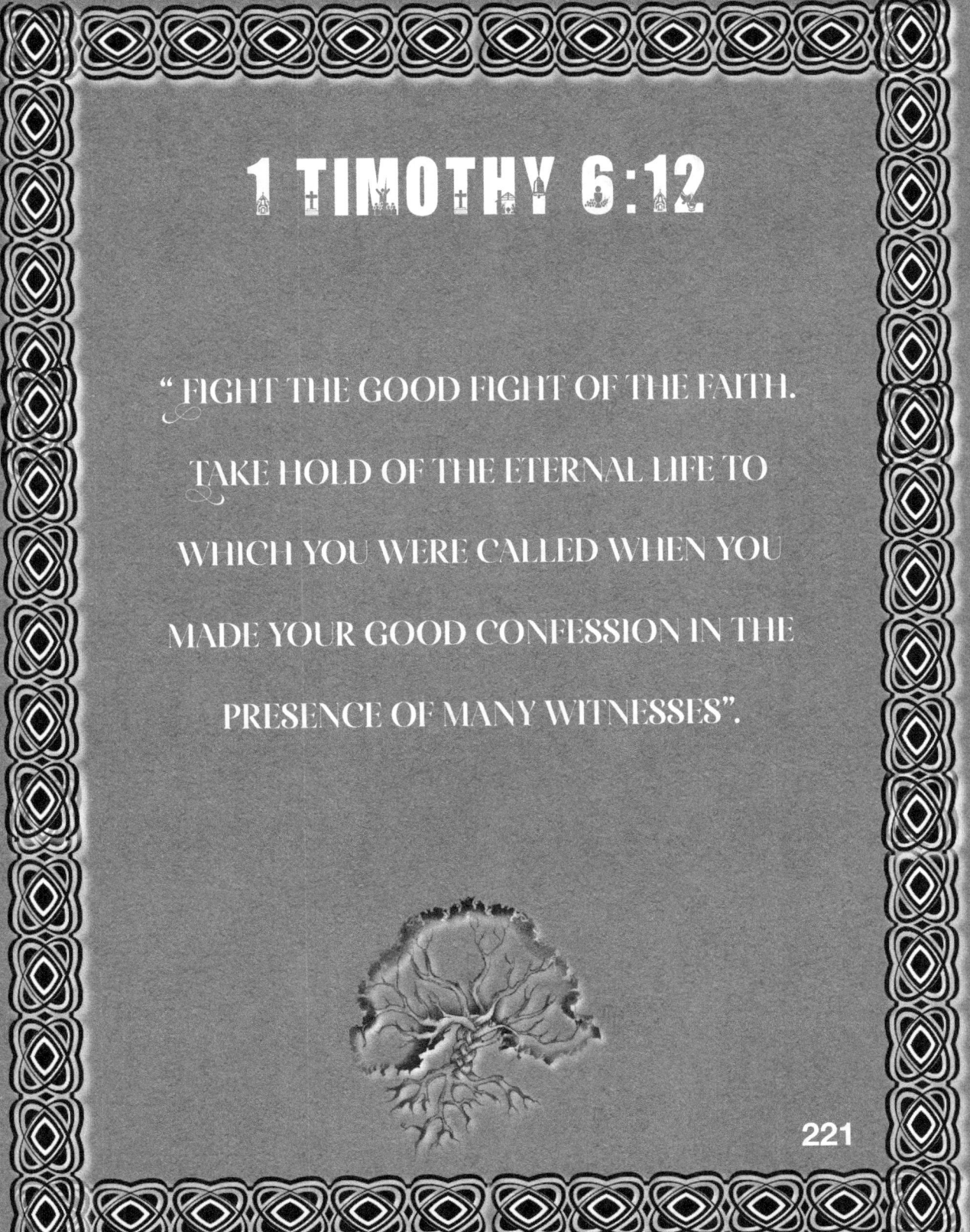

Thank You Lord

 Teach Me

 Guide Me

 # Reflect

Do you feel like you are used all of the talents God gave you this year? If not, what could you change so that you are using them?

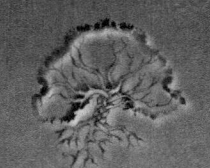
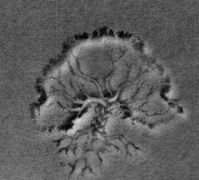

Future Generations

Highlights

My Prayers

 # Prayers

 # Prayers

Prayers

Prayers